CORRECTIONAL REFORM IN NEW YORK

The Rockefeller Years and Beyond

Barbara Lavin McEleney

Marist College

UNIVERSITY PRESS OF AMERICA

LANHAM • NEW YORK • LONDON

4720 Boston Way
Lanham, MD 20706

3 Henrietta Street
London WC2E 8LU England

Library of Congress Cataloging in Publication Data

McEleney, Barbara Lavin, 1943-
Correctional reform in New York.

Bibliography: p.
Includes index.
1. Corrections—New York (State)   I. Title.
HV9475.N6M35   1985   365'.9747   85-17918
ISBN 0-8191-4947-0 (alk. paper)
ISBN 0-8191-4948-9 (pbk. : alk. paper)

DEDICATION

To Jim

ACKNOWLEDGEMENTS

This book would not have been possible had it not been for the support of many who never tired of hearing me discuss the political issues involved in correctional policy making. To all who listened, encouraged and gave of their time and expertise, I am indebted, especially Steve David, Francis Canavan S.J., John Martin and Conrad Rutkowski of Fordham University and to all those interviewed during the course of this research.

A very special thank-you must also be given to James C. McEleney, a true scholar, whose life is dedicated to a quest for knowledge and understanding of man's creativity. For intellectually stimulating and expansive discussions into the wee hours of the morning, for having faith in my scholarly abilities and for not noticing when my share of household chores was left undone, I thank him from the bottom of my heart.

Thanks is also due to M. Nawal Lutfiyya whose expertise on the computer greatly facilitated the preparation of this manuscript into book form.

TABLE OF CONTENTS

PREFACE

This book is a case study of the politics of decision making with regard to correctional policy in New York State, especially during the administration of Governor Nelson A. Rockefeller and updated to 1984.

The activities of various interest groups, namely, the correctional bureaucracy, religious/social reformers, business/labor interests and prison inmates are examined to assess their level and mode of involvement and their relative effectiveness in achieving their goals. The areas examined for such activity include the legislative arena, executive reorganizational schemas, riots and demonstrations within the prisons of Auburn and Attica, and court involvement in issues of prisoner rights.

The findings indicate that the responsiveness of the political system to the demands of such powerless groups as prison inmates was largely symbolic (appeasing but ineffectual), while the powerful, organized correctional bureaucracy received tangible or real benefits.

The study finally raises questions about the limitations of, or modifications necessary in, pluralist theory as a description of New York State correctional politics.

CHAPTER I

BRIEF HISTORY OF THE NEW YORK STATE PRISON SYSTEM

1790-1959

Francis A. Allen has stated that the most salient issues in criminal justice are not those relating to psychiatry, sociology or social psychology. "On the contrary, the most fundamental problems are those of political philosophy and political science. . . . In short, a study of criminal justice is fundamentally a study in the exercise of political power." (1)

Accordingly, this book is an attempt to examine the exercise of political power by those involved in the correctional arena during Nelson A. Rockefeller's term as Governor of New York State, (1959-1973). While this was a period of change, inmate unrest and, eventually, riot which challenged the political authority of Rockefeller's administration and his image as concerned problem solver, he was not the first to be faced with such problems. Historically, conflict between inmates and prison administrators had occurred in a seemingly endless series of recurring strife between the keepers and the kept. Riots had occurred during periods both of custodial ascendancy and rehabilitative ascendancy and the issues were continually the same - namely, humane living conditions and the right to a fair system of justice - rights assumed basic to any citizen of New York.

A brief history of the penal system in New York will provide the backdrop to the specific developments in the 1960s and 1970s with which this study is primarily concerned.

Historical Overview

In the United States, prior to the 1790s, prisons were used primarily as housing for vagrants, paupers and accused offenders prior to trial. They were not used as punishment per se, since convicted colonial offenders were usually whipped publicly, branded, mutilated, hanged or banished - methods of punishment derived from England's severe criminal codes. (2)

However, cultural and social influences led to the assessment of these forms of punishment as cruel, barbaric and unscientific. Such a novel assessment can be traced to the eighteenth century which witnessed a movement from the abstract, philosophical thought centered in the Church, to the pragmatic, factual orientation of men of science. The scientific revolution coincident with the age of discovery and commerce led to a focus on man as originator of ideas. No longer was he considered to be merely a spiritual being, a child of God and hence dependent. Now man was viewed as an intelligent, rational being capable of choice and control of his destiny, hence independent. And this intellectual independence had its ramifications in politics, science and philosophy. The French Revolution perhaps best exemplifies this new found confidence in man's ability to ford new horizons. The French Philosophes: Rousseau, Voltaire, Diderot viewed man as innately good, and hence undeserving of harsh, physical punishments. The growth of statistics as a science enabled man to quantify the facts of social existence and led in turn to a study of man and his behavior - including his unlawful activity.(3) Causes were sought for criminal activity and so causes were found. "Many men became criminals because of adverse economic, environmental or educational circumstances over which they had no control. . . as such they should be given curative treatment."(4)

Thus in 1776, Jonah Hanway drew the plan for one of the first prisons in the New World which would utilize imprisonment for criminal offenders as a rehabilitative device, and not as retributive punishment. The Quakers (Society of Friends), perhaps because they were so often victims of England's criminal justice system, were considered a significant power in the New World, directing the movement toward a theory and policy of rehabilitation.(5) The prison was to accommodate two hundred inmates in cells twenty-four feet deep by twenty feet wide, by fourteen feet high. The keystone of this system, later known as the Pennsylvania Prison System, was solitary confinement for the purpose of spiritual meditation on one's former criminal life. It was believed that this solitude would lead to repentance and a resolve not to sin nor offend again. Accordingly, each cell was connected to a central chapel by an individual enclosed passageway terminating in a separate barred opening from which the inmate could observe church services but not his fellow inmates. Tracts and printed sermons were distributed to the inmates and spiritual needs took precedence over any consideration of potential gain which might accrue to the state from inmate labor. (Inmates performed some labor at a single workbench in their cells.) Individual walled gardens were provided for the physical exercise of the inmates and were reached by passageways similar to those leading to the chapel.(6)

Anonymity pervaded the Pennsylvania institution to the greatest degree possible. Prisoners were unknown to each other, outsiders and guards except by number. Breaches of discipline were punished by confinement in a dungeon on a diet of bread and water. Thus, from the beginning, we see the coexistence of custody and corrections, discipline and rehabilitation which David Rothman has described so well in his work on the history of

2

incarceration. (7)

But the Pennsylvania Model, still in the early stages of growth, soon became discredited due to the numerous cases of insanity which seemed to accompany prolonged solitary confinement. In addition, the unproductivity of prisoners and the relatively spacious cells proved costly. Thus, New York was to modify and later greatly change (with the construction of Auburn Prison) many aspects of the Pennsylvania Model. (8)

Newgate Prison, built in 1796, was the first prison constructed in New York State. It incorporated many of the "reform ideas" of the original Pennsylvania Model, thanks to Thomas Eddy, a New York Quaker. Religious education and worship were encouraged at Newgate and a night school was established but with attendance restricted to the well-behaved. (9) To avoid the insanity associated with solitary confinement, inmates were housed and fed in congregate fashion. Worship and labor were also in common with solitary confinement used only as a disciplinary measure. (10)

Contrary to the situation which evolved later in the early 1900s where prison administrators were virtually autonomous rulers, at this early stage, many public and political officials were involved in the formulation and administration of penal policy. In this regard, an interesting parallel can be drawn to the active court involvement of the 1970s and 1980s. But let us not get too far ahead of our story.

Responsibility for Newgate Prison was divided among numerous political officials: all the Justices of the State Supreme Court, the State Attorney General and Assistant Attorney General, the Mayor and the Recorder of New York City and seven Inspectors. The Inspectors appointed an agent whose primary concern was the financial and industrial operation of the prison and a principal keeper who was the chief disciplinary official. (11) Thus, we see the aspect of public accountability which would soon be lost amid more pragmatic concerns for an efficient and secure operation.

Overcrowding, a major concern in the 1980s was also a problem for the administrators of the 1800s. Riots occurred in 1799, 1800 and 1803. To prevent more riots and ease overcrowding, the practice arose of pardoning each year nearly as many convicts as were admitted to keep the overcrowding from reaching intolerable proportions. (12) In addition, an inmate's term of sentence could be reduced by one-quarter for good behavior and a satisfactory production record. And once the population of an institution exceeded 450 inmates, the Governor was authorized, by the New York State Legislature, to employ

3

these inmates "in any way he deemed proper". (13) Thus, inmates worked on the building of new state prisons and canal construction in upstate New York. As a further incentive to diligence, twenty percent of all convict earnings over and above the cost of his keep were to be set aside for the prisoner or his family upon his release. (14) However, a downturn in the economy (Panic of 1819), which resulted in the cancellation of many prison contracts, combined with public pressure for a prison system that would pay for itself without reliance on the tax revenues of the law-abiding and a swing to a more punitive approach soon spelled defeat for such rehabilitative measures. Thus this early form of work release was soon abandoned, not to be reinstated until 1968 by legislative fiat.

At this time, it was also proposed by religious and social reformers, such as the Quakers, that inmates be classified according to severity of crime, age, health and number of previous imprisonments. Theoretically, each group of inmates was to be segregated from every other and receive individualized treatment. Religion and remedial education were viewed as the means of resocializing the inmate into law - abiding society. However, overcrowding of prison facilities never permitted a comprehensive system of classification.

Rioting and prison unrest continued with further modifications of the Pennsylvania Model. In 1817, the Legislature prescribed the death penalty for any inmate who committed arson or assaulted an officer with intent to kill. In 1819, flogging was legalized as a means of penal discipline and stocks and irons were also permitted. (15) It is ironic that the harsh penal punishments decried earlier were now used to bolster the rehabilitative ideal. The conflict between treatment and punishment, present from the beginning of the New York State prison system, was to continue to modern times. (16)

The creation of a new state prison to alleviate the overcrowding at Newgate was authorized by the Legislature in 1816. Influential Republican interests in the Legislature dictated the City of Auburn as the prison site, thereby rewarding their supporters in western New York State with an influx of state money and jobs in the construction, maintenance and administration of the prison. (17) An outgrowth of the Newgate and Pennsylvania Models, Auburn was to modify and eventually greatly reverse many of the reform aspects of the Pennsylvania Prison System.

Administration of the prison at Auburn was streamlined, eliminating the Court Justices, Attorneys General and other public officials. Five inspectors supervised the prison and appointed an agent who also served as principal keeper, thus uniting

4

administrative and disciplinary functions in one office. Eventually control would rest with only one person, the Warden, and he would be able to run his institution and grounds virtually as a fiefdom. Public accountability, present at Newgate was much less a force at Auburn.

The Auburn Model was to reflect in part the character of the residents of Auburn, two of whom were employed as Prison Warden and Principal Keeper. Auburn had been settled by New England emigrants, an agricultural middle class of people who believed strongly in law, hard labor and the establishment of churches and schools. "The campaign to circulate Bibles, to found Sunday schools, to encourage temperance and to enforce Sabbath observance spurted suddenly here."(18)

Allied to the beliefs of the Auburn residents was the growing conviction that a prison must be self-supporting, paying for itself through the labor of its inmates. The Pennsylvania Model with its large individual cells and walled gardens and the inefficient labor of its inmates was costly to build and maintain. All of these factors led to the modifications which became known as the Auburn System, the generally accepted model of most future prisons in the New World to present times.

The most distinctive feature of the Auburn System was its virtual rejection of the rehabilitative ideal. In its stead, primarily, was a pragmatic concern for custody, security and financial solvency.

Individual cells at Auburn were seven feet long, three and one-half feet wide and seven feet high - approximately one-fortieth the size of the Pennsylvania cells. Auburn cells were arranged back to back and in tiers five cells high. The tiers of cells were arranged as an island in the center of the structure with a vacant area eleven feet wide surrounding all four sides of the "island". Enclosing the island and the area around it was an outer shell pierced by small windows affording some degree of light. It was thus, a prison within a prison, for an outside wall surrounded the entire institution.(19) This physical plan then became the model for all New York State maximum security institutions.

All prisoners were to receive the same treatment. Individual classification and treatment of inmates were disregarded. Inmates were virtually isolated from the outside world. All inmates wore black and white striped outfits, were forbidden to receive or write letters and were forbidden visitors except that citizens who paid a fee could come to the prison and view the inmates. These visits by six to eight thousand persons a year at a fee of twenty-five cents per person greatly augmented

5

prison coffers.(20)   Reading material was limited to a Bible or
prayer book.

To maintain discipline and order, a strict silence code
prevailed at all times, even at meals. The inmate was never to
communicate in any way with fellow inmates and elaborate
techniques for constant surveillance, coercion and intimidation
were viewed as a necessary ingredient of security. Some of these
techniques were a result of the military experiences of the
Auburn Prison staff who had served in the War of 1812.(21)

Marching manoeuvres, such as the lock step whereby
inmates marched single file each placing his right hand on the
shoulder of the man in front of him, were used to transfer
inmates from one part of the institution to another. Maintaining
an erect posture, all eyes had to be kept on the keepers who
looked for any movement of lips. Flogging was also a part of the
prison discipline. The classification of guards, later known as
"correction officers", as Lieutenants, Sergeants and Captains in
the upper ranks again serves to confirm the para-military
organization of the prison - a legacy which holds true in the
1980s.

Michel Foucault makes an interesting analogy between this
mechanization of human behavior and the mechanization discovered
in nature by the men of science. The following statements by
Foucault thus clarify the eighteenth century legacy of science and
the resultant deterministic view of man (a quest for cause-effect
sequences) as it is reflected in penal policy. Foucault states,

> Side by side with the major technology of
> the telescope, the lens and the light
> beam, which were an integral part of the
> new physics and cosmology, there were
> minor techniques of multiple and
> intersecting observations. . . preparing
> a new knowledge of man. These (human)
> 'observatories' had an almost ideal model:
> the military camp. In the perfect camp,
> all power would be exercised solely
> through exact observation; each gaze
> would form a part of the overall
> functioning of power.(22)

Bentham's Panopticon was thus to form the theoretical base for a
policy of control, of power over the kept.(23) The Inspectors'
Report of Auburn Prison in 1822 was to reaffirm the preeminence
of control over treatment. "The great end and design of criminal
law is the prevention of crimes, through fear of punishment; the
reformation of offenders being a minor consideration."(24)

6

As mentioned earlier, advocates of the Auburn System believed that the prisons should be self-supporting and provide for their own food, clothing, medical expenses and staff salaries. (25) By 1825, it became the stipulated duty of all New York prison agents to "cause all the expenses of any kind to be supported wholly or as nearly as practicable by the labor of the inmates." (26)

The promulgation of prison self-sufficiency was an indication of a harsher prison policy. Profit sharing or payments to the inmates for extra work was frowned upon. The sections of the Prison Law of 1817 which provided for monetary inducements and time off for good behavior were ignored. A general pessimism as to the possibility of change in an inmate's behavior coupled with the concentrated effort on labor led the prison officials to oppose any education or religious training. The clergy were discouraged from interfering in prison matters.

The Auburn system of prison management with its emphasis on economic solvency(27) and custodial security while disregarding education or religion as a means of resocializing prisoners became the model of all maximum security institutions in New York State, and throughout most of the United States. The Auburn system was and is a punitive system espousing punishment as its cornerstone. (28) As one penal official noted in the Annual Report of the New York State Department of Efficiency and Economy of 1915:

> In some prisons, dungeon cells and bad food brutalize the inmates, while in others the efforts of sentimentalists have produced a condition where men who have committed serious crimes against the society are treated with the most distinguished consideration. . . . Large associations of sincere and sympathetic men and women are continually agitating in favor of more privileges for the criminal population. . . .
>
> In my judgment. . . sanitary cells, good food, and a reasonable amount of recreation should be furnished but the sentence of "imprisonment at hard labor" should be strictly enforced. . . . No punishment is too severe for lazy and rebellious convicts. . . . The idea that these convicts are merely unfortunate victims of social conditions is erroneous. . . . They are almost all

7

vicious, lazy, degenerates but little above the level of the brute in mentality, glorying in their criminal achievements and returning to the company of their kind as soon as released from the prisons. Society owes no consideration to such as these.(29)

The religious beliefs of the Quakers that the convict was an erring child of God to be restored to health by education and religion no longer significantly influenced the penal system. The Auburn system remains in existence in the 1980s and will be examined in greater detail in the following chapters.

Despite the continued survival of the Auburn Model, throughout its history several attempts have been made to change or modify this system. Four types of groups sought change. Two groups exemplified by the religious and social reformers and inmate organizations tried to restore the humanitarian, educational and religious ideals expressed in the Pennsylvania system. Two other groups exemplified by the business and labor interests of the nineteenth century and the custodial interests of the Wardens and prison guards, the correctional bureaucracy, will illustrate the countervailing forces inhibiting reform. These diverse groups are prototypes of the later interest group activity in the New York State prison system during Nelson A. Rockefeller's term as Governor. An historical discussion of their political involvement in the system will thus provide a necessary background for the subsequent chapters.

Religious/Social Reformers

The earliest social and religious reformers involved in the prison system, as noted earlier, were the Pennsylvania Quakers. Their influence soon spread to New York where they were joined by such groups as: The Salvation Army, Volunteers of America, National Council on Crime and Delinquency (1907), Community Service Society (1848) and the New York Prison Association (1844). In general, these prominent New York citizens(30) ruled out vengeance or retribution as an object of imprisonment. They preferred to view the criminal as a social misfit who had been either psychologically or environmentally determined to a criminal life style because of an emotional or physical deficiency. They supported a policy of rehabilitation of criminal offenders which emphasized remedial education, vocational training and psychological counseling.(31)

And many of their reform proposals were incorporated into various study commission reports. It was suggested, for example, that the state secure employment for paroled prisoners

8

and in reality practically guarantee the good conduct of the men through a parole officer. Work release was recommended, whereby a prisoner would be gainfully employed in the community during the day and return to prison every night or on weekends to serve out the remainder of his sentence.(32)

Disparity of prison sentences was also criticized by the reformers. Pre-sentence reports can be traced to a 1915 suggestion that the sentencing Judge be furnished with all of the facts surrounding the crime and the criminal's previous character. Another proposal would have taken sentencing entirely away from the Judge and committed it to a board composed of a lawyer, physician and psychologist aided by a field force which would investigate the prisoner's history, his degree of responsibility, education, concept of morality, possibility of reform, temperament and crime committed(33) - a proposal still in vogue in the 1980s.

Throughout New York history and continuing into the 1980s, there was almost no classification system in the state prison system despite reform demands. Tubercular inmates were sent to Clinton Prison in Dannemora where a special hospital wing was established. Great Meadow received first offenders and those who could profit from a less severe, less secure institution; Auburn Prison received the most difficult prisoners. Classification has always been more concerned with segregation of offenders according to degrees of "dangerousness" rather than according to educational or employment deficiencies. Reformers were always more concerned with the latter, while prison staff were always more concerned with the former.

A synopsis of reform ideals is found in the following statements from a 1931 Report of the Commission to Investigate Prison Administration and Construction.

> New York State should develop a prison system which will protect society from the criminal and his evil deeds by endeavoring to re-educate and retrain the men and women in prison so. . . they may become useful members of the community.(34)

The authors of the Report called for an end to mass treatment and its replacement with a system of constant personal study, individual treatment and training of every prisoner.

> Individual prisoners must be studied by specialists to determine the personality and ability of each, the defects which led to crime and whether or not the

9

individual can through treatment and training be helped to correct or cure these defects.(35)

Thus, by 1931, the mental health model of treatment(36) was firmly espoused. Emphasis was placed on the classification of inmates

> accomplished through carrying over to the prison the methods for diagnosis used in modern hospital and mental clinics; together with the adaptation of the system of testing industrial fitness used by modern industry and adding a case study of early life and environment of the type which welfare agencies have found effective in their efforts to assist the aged and dependent.(37)

The 1931 Report contains additional findings: that the state build no more fortress prisons; that Sing Sing and Attica be made Reception Centers at which a physical and mental examination by a physician, psychologist, psychiatrist and psychiatric social worker would be given to each inmate. The inmate's training assignment and prison assignment would be made on the basis of information gleaned from the medical reports. Six months after admission, the case of each inmate would be reviewed to see if he had made any progress and determine if a change of assignment was warranted. A Board of Progress in each prison would review the case of every inmate at least once a year during the remainder of his term.

It was further proposed that: a medium security prison be built in 1931; the medium secure road camps be continued and extended; experiments in prison housing - small pre-parole units be set up; a psychiatrist be assigned to every prison staff to review progress of inmates. Because this Report of 1931 is the last major reform piece prior to the various reports of the 1960s, it might be well to review the progress made by the reform interests to this date.

Some advances had been made early in reform history: the introduction of commuting sentences for good behavior, provision of a small sum of money for the inmate upon release from prison and the appointment of agents (parole officers) to assist discharged inmates. Elmira Reformatory had been completed in 1877 to house younger and "less vicious" prisoners in a medium security setting without bars or elaborate walls where industries could provide valuable training. Elmira Reformatory, however, had proven to be a disappointment and a punitive regimentation,

10

a legacy of the maximum security prisons, had been carried over to Elmira Reformatory. (38)

The reformers did succeed in the construction of a medium security institution at Wallkill, New York in 1931. The second medium security prison proposed in 1931 however had yet to be constructed or planned in 1959. The experiments in pre-parole housing were still being discussed in February 1968 at the Senate and Assembly Ways and Means Committee Hearings on the Budget requests of the Department of Correction. It was further proposed in 1931 that twenty-five percent of the prison population be housed in medium security prisons. Nevertheless, in 1959, there were approximately nine thousand adult males housed in maximum security prisons in New York State and only one medium security institution existed (at Wallkill) housing approximately five hundred adult male inmates. (See Table 2)

Since the 1790s, reformers had expounded on the importance of education as a rehabilitative tool, yet, in 1930, only six percent of the inmates at Auburn were enrolled in general education classes, thirteen percent of the inmates at Clinton in Dannemora and twenty - three percent at Sing Sing. (39) The State Department of Correction employed only six teachers and paid them about the same salary as the prison guards and maintenance workers. (40) Inmates received instruction in elementary subjects for one and one-half hours per day and most of the teaching was performed by inmates and, in some cases, by guards. (41)

By 1959 there were approximately thirty-six total rehabilitative positions in the adult male prisons of New York State while custodial staff numbered 1,691 guards, or approximately seventy-eight percent of the total personnel in each maximum security prison. Rehabilitative personnel accounted for approximately 1.5 percent of the total staff positions, (42) as indicated in Table 1.

Despite the activities of the reformers, the system remained basically unchanged when Nelson A. Rockefeller assumed leadership of the State in 1959. The size and composition of the prison cells had not changed in 150 years. The silence system prevailed, isolating inmates from one another and communication with the world outside the prison. Security was the major preoccupation of guards and administration while education and counseling were given token recognition. Moreover, in 1960, inmates were confined to their cells fifty percent longer than the inmates confined two hundred years before when the proponents of the Pennsylvania Model constructed the first prison. (43) There were no full time psychiatric services provided inmates in the state prisons. Inmate teachers were still supplementing

11

professional teachers in the institutions.

Inmate Organizations

Inmate organizations formed an important interest group in the 1960s and 1970s. Nevertheless, the first inmate organization (and the only one publicly acknowledged as far as can be determined) was formed at Auburn Prison in 1913. Titled the "Mutual Welfare League", the motto was "Do Good - Make Good". The League was essentially an inmate disciplinary body that guaranteed good order and good conduct of its members in return for certain privileges from the prison administration.(44) Such privileges involved the freedom of the prison yard from five to six thirty o'clock every evening without guard escort, marching to dinner without guard escort, and recommendations to the Warden of trusted prisoners to work on highway details. A grievance committee heard complaints by the inmates for violations of rules, treatment by officers, and quality of food. With sufficient reason, the matter might then be taken up with the Warden. The League acted as an intermediary between the inmates who were members and the prison administration. The League itself handled the discipline of its members usually through loss of privileges.

In its ideal form, the League was to give the inmates experience in self government. It would make inmates "not good prisoners, but good citizens. . . (and) fit them for the free life to which, sooner or later, they would return."(45) Nevertheless, the League was never seriously implemented and soon met its demise at Sing Sing Prison in 1929 when a prison riot gave the guards and administration the opportunity to abolish it.(46) This experiment in self governing had been eliminated earlier in the other state prisons.

Business/Labor Interests

As mentioned earlier, the involvement of business and labor interests in the prison system was inevitable. It has already been noted that the Pennsylvania model with its emphasis on solitary confinement and individual labor in one's cell was inefficient and costly regarding the labor output. In New York State, in both the Newgate and Auburn Prisons, the inmates worked together in shops at prison industries. The proposition that a prison must be self-supporting was ingrained in the Auburn System. The labor of the inmates was thus used to pay for prison expenses.(47)

Originally each individual prison administration bought raw materials, instructed the inmates in the manufacture of such goods and eventually sold the product on the open market.

12

However, prison industry in this form soon floundered, due to poor economic management, unsettled commercial conditions and overcrowding of the prisons which made working conditions difficult. Prison-made goods were competing on an open market with goods manufactured by persons who could analyze the supply and demand flow of the market. Prison officials found they were losing money and there was often no market for their finished prison-made goods. To take the financial burden of prison industry away from the inexperienced prison officials, the Legislature of 1817 required inmates to "work only on raw materials brought to the prisons by private entrepreneurs who agreed to pay a fixed labor charge to have them made into manufactured goods."(48) The private entrepreneurs thus bore the burden of cost of raw materials and the possible hazard of securing a market for the finished product.

Accordingly, it was the duty of prison administrators to find businessmen willing to put their raw materials into the hands of convicts to be later marketed at the risk of business. Low labor rates were offered as an inducement. "By 1826, almost a dozen contracts had been signed at Auburn involving such crafts as coopering, tailoring, shoe making, weaving, tool making and rifle manufacturing."(49) The inmate became an economic slave.

In time, prison workshops were bitterly criticized by the free artisans of New York who viewed prison labor as unfair competition. Restrictive legislation was passed and manufactured goods were required to be labeled "state prison" with the hope that such a label would discourage consumers from purchasing goods made in such an "ominous" place.(50)

The political pressure by the artisans for stringent prison labor laws continued and was successful. The Legislature of 1835 decreed that "no inmate was to be taught any mechanical trade other than the making of an article which usually had to be imported into the country.(51) Seven years later, it was decided that "no convict. . . shall be permitted to work. . . at any other mechanical trade than that which. . . such convict had learned and practiced prior to his conviction."(52) As a result, many existing contracts were declared null and void by the State Attorney General and a new means of employing convicts had to be devised. The restrictive labor laws were having an ill effect on the economy of the prison institutions and many were showing a deficit.

Prison training in a particular skill was also discouraged. Many artisans refused to hire any ex-convict. Having been trained in one of the prison industries, the ex-convict had no choice but to seek employment from the same artisans who had been opposed to the less expensive prison-made goods. Thus the finding of viable employment for convicts without adverse effect on free artisans was a constant problem. It was thus suggested that prisoners be employed only in trades which would not compete with domestic artisans, or in areas where American manufacturers could not meet the demands for goods.(53) In fact, the very choice of location for Clinton Prison, begun in 1845 in one of the most remote areas of northern New York State (Dannemora) was made primarily to secure a new non-competitive market for prison labor, namely the production of iron.(54)

Also, the increasing number of inmates, many of whom were unskilled, resulted in the spoiling of raw materials. Some of the spoiling was a deliberate form of sabotage.(55) This situation coupled with the lack of skilled craftsmen to instruct the inmates and the pressure of restrictive legislation with the public's hesitancy to spend any more money in developing prison industry soon doomed the practice of penal self-support. Prisons became more and more dependent on emergency legislative appropriations.

In 1847, prison industry took a new turn - the production of state-use products, whereby inmates were used in producing supplies for publicly owned institutions. This production eventually became the mainstay of the New York penal industry. The new system of state-use required all state departments and governmental subdivisions to purchase supplies from the prisons. Nevertheless, this source of labor demand did not compensate for the diminution of contract labor which ended totally in 1897 and so prison industry declined. By the end of the nineteenth century, less than one-third of the convicts were at work in the New York prisons.(56) Prisons once again had become dependent on general funds from state coffers.

It is interesting to note that the business interests apparently raised no opposition to the series of restrictive legislation regarding prison labor. This was probably due to an alternative and abundant new source of cheap labor - namely, the immigrants of the late nineteenth century. Thus, labor interests, having eliminated competition from prison labor, withdrew permanently from the correctional arena. Business interests likewise had no need for further involvement in prison policy making.

Thus, an overall analysis of business involvement in the prison system would find it to have been essentially anti-reform. Manufacturing interests supported and encouraged the development and expansion of prison industry because it provided a source of cheap labor for its manufactured goods.(57) Therefore, prison industries expanded to the detriment of educational and rehabilitative efforts. Coincidentally, labor interests were also classified as anti-reform because of their

14

efforts to cut off even legitimate forms of industry used to train inmates for a job upon release. Labor interests were one of the many factors inhibiting an ex-convict from securing legitimate employment upon release.

Correctional Bureaucracy

A fourth interest involved in correctional policy has been the group most immediately concerned with security within the institutions - the prison guards, now known as correctional officers. The custodial interests have become formalized by the unionization of correctional officers into Council 82 of the American Federation of State, County and Municipal Employees. Their participation in the system will be further explored in the following chapters. However, we may note in passing that the impact of their interests in the prison system can be demonstrated by the large expenditures of money for additional custodial staff, locking devices and the intactness of the maximum security system.(58)

Allied with this group and also classified as anti-reform would be those real estate and construction interests who would benefit from the building of large maximum security prisons. The Report of the Commission to Investigate Prison Administration and Construction in 1931 noted the "unnecessarily high" prison construction costs on New York State prisons due, not so much to prices of labor and material, but to "elaborate construction equipment". Critical of decorative columns and arches, cut stone pillars, ornate trim and brick work, the Commission noted particularly the "esthetic" thirty foot wall, six thousand feet long, curved inward at the top, and supposed to be insurmountable being built at Attica.(59) In addition, $600,000 was spent for locking devices on Attica cells.

A 1932 Report noted, "the centuries of overemphasis on discipline and punitive aspects of correctional work. . . the overemphasis on the construction of buildings. . . little or no attention given to the employment of trained personnel." (60)

Between 1932 and 1959, conditions remained basically unaltered. A Report of the New York State Finance Committee written forty years later and entitled, "A Review of Various Aspects of the New York State Correctional Program" supports the conclusions of the 1932 Report.

Such then were the general conditions and policies of the New York prison system due to the influences of the various interest groups and ideologies when Nelson A. Rockefeller was elected Governor of New York in 1958. The period of his administration was to be marked by various administrative

15

reorganization schemas in the area of corrections, conferences on crime and prison riots at Auburn and Attica. We will now proceed to the central analysis of this study, namely, the activities of the various interest groups and the political outcomes in correctional policy during the Rockefeller years 1959-1973.

1. Francis A. Allen, The Borderland of Criminal Justice (Chicago: University of Chicago Press, 1964), pp. 35-36.

2. Harry Elmer Barnes, The Story of Punishment Second Edition Revised (Montclair, N.J.: Patterson Smith, 1930, 1972) and David J. Rothman, The Discovery of The Asylum (Boston: Little Brown and Co., 1971) pp. 48-53.

3. Michel Foucault, Discipline and Punish (New York: Random House. Vintage Books, 1979) Especially Part two, chapters 1 and 2.

4. W. David Lewis, From Newgate to Dannemora: The Rise of the Penitentiary in New York 1796 - 1848 (Ithaca: Cornell University Press, 1965) p. 21. Quotation by John Bellers, an early Quaker prison reformer as cited in Lewis.

5. The theory and policy of rehabilitation has been well documented in the following works: David J. Rothman, Conscience and Convenience (Boston: Little Brown and Co., 1980) especially Chapters 2 and 5 and The Discovery of the Asylum. See also, Francis T. Cullen and Karen E. Gilbert, Reaffirming Rehabilitation (Cincinnati, Ohio: Anderson Publishing Co., 1982), especially, chapters 2 and 3. and Karl Menninger, M.D., The Crime of Punishment (New York: The Viking Press, 1966) for a less theoretical approach to rehabilitation as penal policy.

6. Lewis, From Newgate to Dannemora, p. 26.

7. Rothman, Discovery of the Asylum and Conscience and Convenience. This is a theme that runs through both works.

8. Gustave de Beaumont and Alexis de Toqueville, On the Penitentiary System in the United States and its Applications in France (Carbondale: Southern Illinois University Press, Reprint, 1964) chapter 2, pp. 53-79. See also, Martin D. Schwartz et al. Corrections: An Issues Approach (Cincinnati: Anderson Publishing Co., 1980), Chapter 1, pp. 16-23.

9. Lewis, From Newgate to Dannemora, p. 32.

10. Ibid., pp. 30-31

11. Ibid., p. 35

12.   Barnes, The Story of Punishment, p. 133.

13.   Lewis, From Newgate to Dannemora, p. 44.

14.   Ibid., p. 45

15.   Ibid., p. 46.

16.   This conflict between treatment and punishment is well documented in Rothman, Conscience and Convenience, Chapter 5.

17.   Lewis, From Newgate to Dannemora, p. 54.

18.   Ibid., p. 74.

19.   Ibid., p. 67.

20.   Ibid., p. 124.

21.   Ibid., pp. 86-87.

22.   Foucault, Discipline and Punish, p. 171.

23.   Foucault describes the cultural origins of the Panopticon ideal in Discipline and Punish, Chapter 3, Part 3.

24.   Inspectors' Report of 1822 as quoted in Lewis, From Newgate to Dannemora, p. 63.

25.   Ibid., p. 100.

26.   Ibid.

27.   de Beaumont and de Toqueville, On the Pentitentiary System in the United States, Chapter 4, pp. 108-111.

28.   de Toqueville noted "The Philadelphia system produces more honest men and that of New York (Auburn system) more obedient citizens" in On the Pentitentiary System, p. 91.

29.   Annual Report of the New York Department of Efficiency and Economy (Albany: J.B. Lyon Co., 1915) General Introduction, pp. xxi-xxii.

30.   The philosophical and social background of these reformers, especially in regard to juveniles, is well documented in Anthony M. Platt, The Child Savers (Chicago: University of Chicago Press, 1969) Chapter 4.

31.   Cullen and Gilbert, Reaffirming Rehabilitation, Chapter 3.

32. Annual Report of the New York Department of Efficiency and Economy, 1915, p. 784.

33. Ibid., p. 787

34. Report of the Commission to Investigate Prison Administration and Construction (Albany, February 15, 1931), Introduction, p. 1.

35. Ibid., p. 2

36. For an interesting discussion of the influence of psychiatry on the criminal justice system, see Michel Foucault, I, Pierre Riviere (Lincoln: University of Nebraska Press, 1975) and Willard Gaylin, M.D., The Killing of Bonnie Garland (New York: Penguin Books, 1982).

37. Report of the Commission to Investigate Prison Administration and Construction, Feburary 15, 1931, p. 4.

38. Austin MacCormick, The Education of Adult Prisoners (New York: National Society of Penal Information, 1931) pp. 288-290.

39. Report of the Commission to Investigate Prison Administration and Construction, February 15, 1931, pp. 49-50

40. Ibid., p. 50

41. Ibid., pp. 49-50.

42. New York State Executive Budget. Department of Correction. State Purposes Budget. (New York: State Publication, 1959-60), pp. 151-172.

43. A Review of Various Aspects of the New York State Correctional Program. A report to the New York State Legislature by the Senate Finance Minority. Samuel Greenberg, Chairman. (Greenberg Report) August 29, 1971. Mimeograph. p. 4.

44. Annual Report of the New York Department of Efficiency and Economy, 1915, p. 754. See also, Rothman, Conscience and Convenience, pp. 119-121., and Charles Stastny and Gabrielle Tyrnauer, Who Rules the Joint (Lexington, Mass.: D.C. Heath and Company, 1982) pp. 48-51.

45. Quoted in Rothman, Conscience and Convenience, p. 121.

46. Ibid., p. 131.

47. For a radical interpretation of prison labor see Rosalind P.

19

Petchesky, "At Hard Labor: Penal Confinement and Production in Nineteenth Century America" in Crime and Capitalism, edited by David Greenberg (Palo Alto: Mayfield Publishing Co., 1981) pp. 341-357.

48.   Lewis, From Newgate to Dannemora, p. 44.

49.   Ibid., p. 180

50.   Ibid., pp. 187-188.

51.   Ibid., p. 193.

52.   Lewis, From Newgate to Dannemora, p. 197.

53.   Ibid., p. 198.

54.   Ibid., p. 200.

55.   Ibid., p. 184.

56.   Blake McKelvey, American Prisons (Montclair, N.J.: Patterson Smith, 1968) p. 107.

57.   Lewis, From Newgate to Dannemora, Chapter 8.

58.   Report of the Commission to Investigate Prison Administration and Construction, February 15, 1931, p. 39 and New York State Executive Budget.   Department of Correction, State Purposes Budget, 1959-1960.

59.   Report of the Commission to Investigate Prison Administration and Construction, February 15, 1931, p. 39.

60.   Report of the Commission to Investigate Prison Administration and Construction.   Educational Program Report. (New York State Publication, January 1932), p. 5.

CHAPTER II

THE CORRECTIONAL ARENA, 1959-1965:

Continuation of the Status Quo

Nelson A. Rockefeller was elected Governor of New York State in 1958. His term of office from 1959-1973 was among the longest of recent history and his impact on the state was significant in many areas. Although his policies in the area of narcotics addiction had far reaching ramifications in the correctional arena, as we shall see in the following chapters, it was the Attica Prison riot in 1971 which focused public attention directly on the Governor's penal policy. How did this policy evolve? What were its roots?

One of the first tasks of the new Governor was the appointment of the members of his Cabinet and, in particular, the appointment of the Commissioner of the Department of Correction. Richard McGee has said that this decision may be the most crucial one a Governor may ever make.

> It should be done with extreme care, and if ever he should put aside secondary political considerations, this is the place. His Director of Corrections will need his (the Governor's) constant support, because no matter how competent the director may be, he cannot do the job alone. Especially he will need support in the Legislature. (1)

Nelson A. Rockefeller had a reputation as a pragmatist, a problem solver, one who paid little attention to ideology, one to whom party lines were secondary considerations if the prospective employee or appointee was a competent individual. (2) Once the individual had been chosen, Rockefeller preferred to let his Commissioners handle all of the internal workings of their respective departments. As a former high-level aide has noted:

> The Governor depended heavily on his staff to manage state government and had relatively few dealings with the Commissioners directly. He was not very much interested in administration. He was more concerned with solving problems, putting together big programs; and he depended on his staff to watch

21

the administration, confident that if they ran into a mess, it would be brought to his attention. (3)

Several names no doubt were suggested to Rockefeller in his search for a Commissioner of the Department of Correction. Had the Governor wished to change the orientation of Corrections from one of custody to one of rehabilitation, he might have chosen Russell G. Oswald, lawyer, former social worker and Chairman of the New York State Board of Parole. Previously, Oswald had served as Commissioner of Correction in Wisconsin and Massachusetts. He had the reputation of being a liberal, a reformer and a competent administrator. (4) As Commissioner, Oswald might be expected to make changes and commit the Department of Correction to a policy of rehabilitation of criminal offenders. (5) Most probably, according to insiders in the field, his name was among those suggested to Rockefeller.

On the other hand, the correctional bureaucracy would not have been supportive of a social worker Commissioner. For the most part, the bureaucracy rejected the notion of "rehabilitation". (6) They believed, for the most part, that the offender was one who had deliberately chosen an illegal way of life, had thus offended society and deserved to be punished. (7) This faction supported a punitive correctional policy that emphasized deprivation of liberty through incarceration. Mere custody of inmates and security of the prison institutions were the program components. And the man they would have supported was "one of their own", a former New York State Police Trooper who had worked his way up through the ranks of corrections, Paul McGinnis. Former Governor Averill Harriman, Rockefeller's predecessor, had appointed McGinnis as Commissioner of Correction but had subsequently dismissed him, allegedly for recruiting votes for Rockefeller among correctional personnel. (8) McGinnis enjoyed a law enforcement reputation within and outside the department. (9) Former staff members noted that McGinnis already had a reputation for "keeping expenses down" and "things quiet" within the institutions. (10) As Commissioner of Correction, McGinnis then could be counted upon to appease bureaucratic interests by continuing the status quo and by maintaining rigid control of the institutions.

No doubt other names were also suggested to Rockefeller for consideration. But when Rockefeller appointed Paul McGinnis as Commissioner of the Department of Correction on January 1, 1959, he chose an individual who had proven himself a competent administrator since no riots by inmates, nor demonstrations by guards gave any indication of internal upheaval. There was no reason for Rockefeller to make any changes; things seemed to be going well in the correctional arena. McGinnis' appointment further satisfied Rockefeller's Lieutenant Governor, Malcolm Wilson, an old friend and supporter of McGinnis.(11)

Having come up through the bureaucratic ranks, McGinnis could be expected to share and defend bureaucratic interests and policies, such as on-the-job safety, job security and remuneration and the traditional policy of secure custody. That this particular policy emphasis persevered in the prisons as Rockefeller began his governorship and as McGinnis began his second term as Commissioner is manifested by an examination of the physical plant and staffing distribution in 1959.

Paul McGinnis began his second term as Commissioner with a budget of $40 million to distribute among various institutions and his own administrative staff. McGinnis was in charge of a large bureaucratic structure which encompassed six state prisons for adult males, (five maximum and one medium security), one for adult females, a reception center for males between the ages of 16 and 21 (located at Elmira, New York), two hospitals for the mentally ill offenders and a Youth Rehabilitation Facility, consisting of four conservation work camps.(12) At the time of his appointment in 1959, there were approximately 6,000 personnel positions in the Department of Correction. Since our primary concern is the five maximum and one medium security prisons for adult males,(13) it should also be noted that there were a total of approximately 2,400 personnel positions in these institutions. More than seventy-five percent of these positions were custodial in nature as can be seen from the data in Table 1 (Appendix). For example, in each of the maximum security prisons, the entire rehabilitative staff averaged between five and ten positions (teachers, counselors, chaplains), whereas the custodial staff (correction officers) averaged between 294 and 364 positions.(14) The ratio of custodial to rehabilitative positions was, on an average, 47 to 1 (See Table 1). Inmates in the maximum security prisons for adult males in 1959 numbered approximately 10,000.(15) The average inmate population in each of these prisons was 1,500-2,000 inmates.(16) Only Wallkill, the state's one medium security institution had a smaller number of inmates (495) and a greater number of rehabilitative positions (25). One hundred correction officers were charged with the security of Wallkill Prison,(17) which had been constructed as a reform institution in the 1930s.

The data in Table 2 (Appendix) illustrates the fact that for most of McGinnis' administration, the Correction Department was faced with a declining state prison population. Various reasons have been put forth to explain the decreasing state prison population, among them: changes in the Parole Board's policy regarding releases which resulted in an increase in the number of persons paroled;(18) a decrease in parole violators as a result of improved parole services;(19) and various judicial decisions and higher court actions which resulted in the release of certain groups of inmates from Matteawan and Dannemora State Hospitals for the Criminally Insane.(20) These court actions had mandated the review of the sentences of the criminally insane and in many instances these inmate patients had been transferred to civil mental hospitals.(21)

While the general trend was a declining prison population, there did occur a temporary increase in the prison population between 1960 and 1963 (See Table 2) and whenever the estimated prison population(22) reflected an increase, additional custodial positions were requested and received by the Wardens. Moreover, not only were additional custodial positions requested, but in the Governor's Executive Budget of 1963-1964, funds for the acquisition of land for two new prison insititutions were recommended. One of the proposed institutions was a maximum security prison that would accommodate 1,500 inmates; the other, a reception center to accommodate 800 young male offenders. Governor Rockefeller stated, "the increasing institutional population will soon fill existing facilities and therefore I am recommending funds for the acquisition of land for two new prison institutions."(23) It should be noted that, in fact, by simple arithmetic, a fifteen percent increase in the prison population would have been required to justify construction of a new prison with a capacity of 1,500 inmates. However, there was only a four percent increase in the prison population between 1960 and 1963. Thus Rockefeller's support for these proposed new facilities in view of the contravening data needs to be explained.

According to one former Department official, the proposals for the new prison and reception center stemmed from pressure within the Department of Correction from correction officers (custodial interests) who foresaw increasing security needs concomitant with a changing inmate population - now predominantly composed of Black and Puerto Rican inmates.(24) This new breed of inmate had a reputation within the prisons as being more violent and troublesome than former inmates.

For three years, the proposed plan for the new penal institutions was supported by the Executive administration and Legislative leadership, seemingly without opposition.

Despite the fact that reform interests had long decried the construction of massive prison buildings designed to house 1,500-2,000 inmates, they appear to have voiced no opposition to the aforementioned construction plans. In interviews with several reform group representatives, they stated that they had taken no position in opposition to the construction of the new penal institutions,(25) even though they had long supported a limitation on prison size and adhered to the view of the former Warden of Wallkill Prison, Charles McKendrick, that a prison in order to rehabilitate its offenders should house no more than 500 inmates.(26) It should be noted in passing that McKendrick was an anomaly within the Department. Most Wardens shared the views of the guards that the function of the prison was custody and security. The Society of Friends had also issued a general policy statement supporting a moratorium on the construction of any new penal institutions,(27) but it did not get involved in the New York construction plans.

Plans for the construction of the new penal institutions continued. In 1964, the Legislature approved $160,000 for acquisition of land for the new prisons, despite indications of a declining state prison population in 1964. In retrospect, as can be seen in Table 2, this tendency toward a declining state prison population was to continue into the 1970s. Nevertheless, in 1966-1967, the Capital Construction Appropriation Budget of the Department of Correction included a recommended appropriation of $10 million for construction of the two new penal institutions.(28)

The proposal for the construction of the new prison upstate was linked to the closing of Sing Sing as a prison and its transformation into a Reception/Classification Center which would be able to identify the "troublesome" new inmates of such concern to the prison guards. However, the transformation of Sing Sing into this type of smaller facility would have meant fewer jobs for the guards, most of whom lived in Ossining or in nearby New York City and consequently would have meant their transfer to the prisons upstate, located in remote areas. The prison employees and the business interests of Ossining, where the prison was located, voiced strong opposition to Lieutenant Governor Malcolm Wilson, a resident of Westchester County, in which Sing Sing was located.(29) In this instance, the correction officers of Sing Sing were more concerned with the protection of their own jobs than with any benefit the overall system would have gained from the Reception/Classification Center.

Simultaneously, opposition to the new Center was also voiced by other constituents of Wilson. Linked to the reduction in size of Sing Sing was a transportation plan to build a highway which would have been constructed through the grounds of the prison. Local Westchester residents whose property bordered on the Hudson River feared the new highway would financially and ecologically ruin their property and the surrounding area. They too voiced their opposition to Wilson.

According to John R. Dunne, former Chairman of the New York State Senate Penal Institutions Committee, Wilson's support of both groups of his constituents, namely, the employees of Sing

25

Sing and the property owners, resulted in the retention of Sing Sing as a maximum security prison and subsequently meant the defeat of the prison construction planned for upstate. (30)

Thus, in 1967, the recommended appropriation of $10 million was deleted when the rest of the budget was voted by the Legislature. Later a $1 million recommended appropriation was inserted in the Supplemental Budget to renovate some sections of the older institutions. Rockefeller's acquiesence in Malcolm Wilson's recommendation that Sing Sing not be changed seemed to be payment of a political debt. In political circles, it was generally believed that Rockefeller would not have won the election in 1958 had it not been for Wilson's help in upstate conservative communities. (31)

It is interesting to note that reform interests appeared not to have even known about the proposed Reception/Classification Center nor the building of a new prison upstate. (32) Both of these items were essentially internal budgetary items and the reformers claimed they had no formal access to the budgetary process. They did not know the process, nor the individuals involved, nor were they ever asked for their opinion on budget items, (33) as is seen from a policy analysis of the budgetary process in Corrections.

Budgetary Process/Policy

The budgetary process began in the Department of Correction with the Wardens of each prison institution. (34) Each Warden prepared a line item budget for his institution which noted all of the personnel positions (administrative, educational, psychiatric counseling, religious ministers, custodial, correction officers and maintenance), as well as the costs of maintenance and operation of the prison. Budgets were initially therefore very detailed documents. In the preparation of their budgets, Wardens were essentially mere cost accountants detailing the expenses of maintaining their prisons "as is". Within the hierarchical structure of the correctional bureaucracy, they did not have the authority to redefine their own functions nor to institute fundamental reforms. Such policies, and their funding, would have to be instituted from above, from the administrative office in Albany. Wardens might make suggestions to their superiors at other times; nevertheless in the preparation of their budget, they could really only list the expense of maintaining the status quo. (35) This condition of the Wardens was further reinforced by McGinnis' directives to the Wardens to "keep expenses down." (36)

When the Warden had prepared his budget, he submitted it to the central administration of the Department in Albany. There

26

the heads of various divisions (Administration, Education, Estimate and Audit, Identification, Probation, Youth, Research and the Commission of Correction) would then extract their segments of the institution's budget and when they had reviewed it would, with the Wardens, present the institutional budgets to the Commissioner for final ratification.

The budgetary function of the Divisional heads was again merely that of cost accountants; determining the cost of their programs by amalgamating the relevant sections from the individual budgets of each Warden. The structural limitations of the bureaucracy that applied to the Wardens applied also to the Divisional heads at this juncture.(37) In addition, McGinnis' directive to "keep expenses down" prevented the Divisional heads from formulating innovative rehabilitative programs.

Thus within the Department of Correction, there was in effect a budgetary process which because of its structure did not provide for new programs, but merely for the increment necessitated by salary increases or increased costs relating to the maintenance and operation of the institutions.(38) In sum, maintenance of the status quo was thereby guaranteed, while new policies and programs could not first be expressed in the budgetary process.

When the budget had been approved by the Commissioner, usually in July/August of the year, it was then submitted in September/October to the Governor's fiscal expert and appointee, the Director of the Division of the Budget. During most of Rockefeller's administration, the man who held this post was T. Norman Hurd.(39)

The Division of the Budget consisted of a Director, Deputy Director, five other administrative posts and the Examining units. The Director was appointed by the Governor; the Director's administrative assistants and Deputy Director were appointed by the Director. All of the above were exempt civil service positions. The vast majority of 275 positions in the Division of the Budget were classified as permanent civil service positions.

The functions of the Division of the Budget are statutorily listed: "to correlate and revise estimates and requests for appropriations of the departments and agencies of the State; to assist the Governor in his duties respecting the investigation, supervision and coordination of the expenditures and other fiscal operations of the various departments and agencies."(40)

The personnel within the Division of the Budget were always presented with a completed Departmental budget. They did not participate in the drawing up of the original Departmental

27

budget, although budget examiners during the year sometimes made on-site visits to departmental programs. The Division of the Budget statutorily had no authority to initiate policy, except as it might have been set forth by the Governor. As a governmental bureaucratic structure, the Division of the Budget could only "correlate and revise" fiscal requests made by the Department of Correction.

In addition, the structure of the Division was highly stratified. The Budget examiners who initially reviewed the departmental budgets were supervised by a Deputy Director or Administrative Assistant who in turn received direction from the Director of the Budget who theoretically had in turn received his directives from the Governor. But Rockefeller tended not to get involved in the details of the budgetary process, preferring instead to develop monumental programs much to the consternation of the fiscally conservative civil servants in the Budget Division. As one former staff member has stated,

> (Rockefeller) is very receptive to new ideas - too much so, in my opinion - and his enthusiasm needs to be curbed. . . . The Budget Division tried to discipline Rockefeller by channeling facts and data to him largely through the Director of the Budget, in the belief that yesterday's decisions are today's budget problems. But Rockefeller is very program-oriented and less oriented toward fiscal controls.(41)

Any changes made by the budget examiners had to be approved subsequently by the Deputy Director and Director. This very bureaucratic structure precluded any attempt at innovative and radical change that did not originate with the Governor and in the area of Corrections, the Governor was content to let things be.

As noted earlier, the vast majority of personnel in the Division of the Budget (275 positions) were lifetime career civil servants. In many cases, they had served a variety of administrations, Democratic and Republican. The tendency among Budget personnel was to consider the Division of the Budget as an "apolitical" institution.(42) Also, many of the budget examiners originally had been employed by the Department they were now "examining".(43) For example, John Corrigan, the administrator in charge of the Correction Department Budget for most of the time period under consideration, originally had been employed by the Correction Department and had worked for a total of four years at Napanoch Reformatory and later in the

28

Department's central office in Albany. By 1960, Corrigan had already been in civil service for twenty - six years.(44)

Thus the tendency toward the status quo within the Department of Correction was also perpetuated within the Division of the Budget. As Corrigan has stated,

> It is up to us to finance the programs as economically as possible. . . . We are forced to make major cuts in the Department budgets, because if we didn't, the Department heads would ask for the world.(45)

Within the Division of the Budget, the status quo was maintained and assured by 1) the structure of the budgetary process and 2) politically, by the personnel who staffed the bureaucratic structure.

When all state department budgets had been reviewed, the Director of the Division of the Budget would present the amalgamation of all budgets, the Executive Budget, to the Governor for a final review and confirmation. The final Executive Budget was then presented to the Legislature by the Governor in January.

Informally, it has been asserted that the most influential person in developing correctional budgetary policy was John Corrigan, administrator in charge of reviewing the Correction Department budget for the Division of the Budget. According to a Corrections expert,

> Corrigan, because of his previous experience in Corrections viewed himself as an expert and would arbitrarily cut programs he felt were not satisfactory. . . . He treats state money as if it were his own.(46)

The correction official in charge of the Educational Program in the Department concurred,

> Understanding, sympathy, and expertise were just not there in the Division of the Budget, and they were unwilling to accept the expertise from the Department of Correction. Budget examiners were not knowledgeable and used to tear the budget apart and cut items they did not understand. . . . The Governor did not

exert as strong a hand as he might have.(47)

Ultimately, cuts in the Correction Department budget had at least the tacit approval of the Governor. At this point in the budgetary process, new policies and programs could have been recommended by the Governor. In fact, they were not.

Corrigan has stated that Rockefeller did make some recommendations.(48) However, according to Corrigan,

> The Governor's primary area of interest was the State University System. . . so no special attention was given to the Correction Department Budget. The Governor paid as much attention to Corrections as to any other state agency budget. . . . When things are going smoothly, there is no need to get involved in program change, nor is there any need for the Governor's special involvement.(49)

As Corrigan intimates, the Governor's priority regarding state agencies was obviously a pragmatic maintenance of the status quo in most issue areas, except those receiving special attention. Because Corrections had traditionally been accorded a low priority and there were, in addition, no public riots nor demonstrations within the prisons that demanded Gubernatorial reaction, the Division of the Budget was granted virtual autonomy in the trimming or amendment of the original Correction Department budget.

However, according to other top level administration officials within the Department of Correction, neither the Governor nor the Division of the Budget was responsible for the lack of additional program budget money in Corrections. Former Deputy Commissioner of Corrections, Walter Dunbar, has stated that "neither the Governor nor the Division of the Budget received any program requests from McGinnis".(50) Vito Ternullo, former head of the Division of Education within the Correction Department, has reiterated that "McGinnis saw that the Department was keeping expenses down and was proud of that fact."(51)

The reformers, on their part, did not attempt to exert any pressure regarding the budget. John Corrigan, of the Division of the Budget, has stated that he was never confronted by any of the religious/social reformers; in fact, he had never met any of them.

> I've never had any direct contact with
> reformers, but reformers are not aware of
> the budgetary process. They do not
> know the individuals involved nor do they
> understand the workings of the budgetary
> process. . . . Sometimes when programs
> are cut, reformers attempt to influence
> the budget, but then only through the
> mail. (52)

Senator John R. Dunne has also noted that "reformers were not interested in the budgetary process."(53) And reform groups such as Community Service Society's Committee on Youth and Correction, Osborne Association and Urban Coalition have verified this pattern of budgetary non-involvement.(54)

Thus in the absence of pressure by reformers for funding of rehabilitation programs, the interests of the bureaucracy for security and custody in the form of additional correctional officer personnel were maintained. Former Commissioner of Corrections, Russell G. Oswald, has remarked that departmental policy under McGinnis became "primarily a question of satisfying demands of the correctional officers for security measures". (55)

It is also generally agreed that the Correction Department under McGinnis received what was requested in its budget. Senator John Dunne has verified that the Legislature made very few changes in the Correction Department budget as presented in the Governor's Executive budget. Dunne has stated that "Corrections got what they asked for, which was very little".(56)

Executive and Legislative fiscal policy as it related to corrections may then be characterized as support of the bureaucracy and the maintenance of the status quo.

Legislative Arena

The correctional bureaucracy again were the beneficiaries in the legislative arena.

Throughout this time period, prisoner rights legislation was introduced time and again but ignored, such as the following bills introduced in the 1963 legislative session: restrictions on the use of leg irons in courtroom appearances, freedom of worship to Muslim inmates, increased clothing allowances to released felons, segregation of first offenders from "hardened criminals", extension of the medium security work camps in lieu of incarceration in the maximum security prisons. These bills and others, introduced in subsequent sessions in 1964 and 1965 such as: state assumption of the costs of local confinement of

31

sentenced prisoners, proposals for intensive job training programs and the establishment of psychiatric and diagnostic clinics in the prison system for offenders convicted of violent, sexual or degeneracy crimes were not voted out of the Senate Penal Institutions Committee, nor its Assembly counterpart, for consideration by either the Senate or Assembly.

In some cases, these bills were prevented from reaching the Assembly or Senate floor through a negative vote in committee; in other instances, no action was taken on the bills and hence these bills were said to have "died" in committee. In both cases, the bills were never released from committee for a floor vote by the entire body of Senators or Assemblymen.

One former legislative aide has remarked that the Senators who were chairmen of the Penal Institutions Committee prior to 1967, when Senator John R. Dunne was appointed chairman, never kept files or correspondence on penal issues. All correspondence from inmates was immediately discarded in the waste paper basket.(57) Former Warden Charles McKendrick, a noted liberal and academician (58) and Warden of Wallkill Prison until his death in 1972, had noted that prior to Senator John Dunne's prison visits, he had never had any contact with legislators, had never been asked for any information on prison issues.(59) McKendrick believed that legislative non-interest could be summed up in the dictum, "there are no votes in prison".(60)

Black and Hispanic minorities lacked significant representation in the New York State Legislature and this had an impact on consideration of prisoner rights issues. As Gerald Benjamin has noted, even though there have been more Democrats than Republicans enrolled in New York State in every year since World War II, the Republican Party has been extraordinarily successful in state elections.(61)

> The GOP has controlled the Governorship and the state assembly for all but four years since World War II and has lost dominance of the state senate for only one year.(62) The Republican constituency may be found in traditionally rural Republican areas upstate, suburban areas adjacent to the state's major cities and the growing counties of the lower Hudson Valley.(63)

It has also been noted that,

> Prior to reapportionment in 1964, Republicans enjoyed an advantage in the

state assembly that gave them roughly ten
percent more seats than their proportion
of the total statewide vote would
indicate.(64)

Traditionally the Republicans have polled very few Black or
Hispanic votes (65) and hence did not need to respond to
minority interests. Robert Connery, political essayist of the
Rockefeller administration, had also noted that Republican
legislators from upstate districts were generally not supportive of
liberal social legislation which would have meant increased state
spending and increased taxes antithetical to upstate Republican
interests.(66)

Thus it should be noted that the New York State
Legislature was controlled primarily by rural and suburban
conservative Republican interests, and that minority rights or
prisoner rights legislation was not a concern of their
constituents.

Certainly, the correctional bureaucracy had little interest in
supporting prisoner rights legislation and may even have voiced
opposition to it. Within the Correction Department, it was well-
known that prisoner rights issues met with little sympathy or
understanding. One of McGinnis' administrative assistants has
noted that "McGinnis fought the Muslims tooth and nail. . . . He
just did not understand them."(67) A collective inmate
consciousness had not yet taken form and no public action by way
of demonstrations or riots was taken by inmates as a way of
making known their demands.

In the state legislative arena, as in the budgetary arena,
the reformers were notably absent. There is no record of
reformer support for the numerous pieces of correctional reform
legislation that year after year were introduced in the Legislature
but never voted out of committee. Legislators do not recall any
interest or involvement in correctional matters by the reform
groups.(68) Former Commissioner Russell G. Oswald, active in
the correctional arena since 1957, has stated that "reformers were
not active in penal reform until the radical activists became
involved after the Attica riot in 1971."(69)

The reform groups themselves have noted a lack of
involvement in state correctional reform. For example, the
Community Service Society became actively involved in policy
issues, according to one staff member, "only after 1965, when our
hostels for delinquent youth were being phased out."(70) A
former New York State Director of the National Council on Crime
and Delinquency, has noted the failure of government agencies to
take NCCD seriously.(71) The National Conference of Christians

33

and Jews, despite their involvement in corrections in other states, have concentrated their efforts in New York City on Police - Minority Community Relations work "because this is where we have been accepted."(72)   The Salvation Army and the Society of Friends, preoccupied with ameliorating the physical needs of inmates and ex-offenders, were likewise not involved in legislative or budgetary decision-making.(73)   According to some observers, even the age-old New York Prison Association, renamed the Correctional Association of New York, was not aggressively active in the field of penal reform.(74)

Thus this period of the early and mid 1960s was characterized by a continuation of the status quo and support of custodial interests.   The reformers' lack of involvement, the bureaucratic concern for security and at the same time program economy, together with Rockefeller's lack of interest in this arena, contributed to a reinforcement of the status quo which may be viewed as a continuing tangible allocation of resources to the custodial interests of the correctional bureaucracy.   The changing inmate population, increasingly composed of Black and Puerto Rican minorities, was still quiescent - but not for long.

34

Endnotes - Chapter II

1. Richard A. McGee Prisons and Politics (Lexington, Mass.: D.C. Heath and Co., 1981) p. 26.

2. Robert H. Connery and Gerald Benjamin Rockefeller of New York (Ithaca: Cornell University Press, 1979), p. 12 and p. 27. Barbara A. Lavin - participant observer - 1968-1972

3. Quoted in Connery and Benjamin, Rockefeller of New York, p. 156.

4. Barbara A. Lavin - Participant Observer

5. For additional information on Rehabilitation of Criminal Offenders consult: Rudolph Gerber and Patrick McAnany, eds. Contemporary Punishment (Notre Dame: Notre Dame University Press, 1972) Chapter 5, "Rehabilitation" pp. 175-227; Leon Radzinowicz and Marvin Wolfgang, Crime and Justice. Vol 2: The Criminal in the Arms of the Law Second Edition. (New York: Basic Books., 1977) Parts 1 and 4. For a critique of rehabilitation see Radzinowicz and Wolfgang, Crime and Justice. Vol 3: The Criminal Under Restraint Second Edition. Part 4, articles 24 and 25. For a general introduction to rehabilitative thought see: Francis Cullen and Karen Gilbert Reaffirming Rehabilitation (Cincinnati, Ohio: Anderson Publishing Co., 1982.)

6. Russell G. Oswald, Attica - My Story (Garden City: Doubleday and Co., 1972) p. 152, as follows: "The custodial group in the maximum security institutions says that treatment, euphemistically used, is most effective when it is given under lock and key. The social workers and classification committees see much of their work made ineffective by the custodial group's indifference. Who prevails? Normally it is the security group."
    In addition see: Ben M. Crouch, Editor The Keepers - Prison Guards and Contemporary Corrections (Springfield: Charles C. Thomas, Publisher, 1980) and James B. Jacobs New Perspectives on Prisons and Imprisonment (Ithaca: Cornell University Press, 1983) especially chapters 6-10. Also, Lawrence Hazelrigg, Editor, Prison in Society (Garden City: Doubleday and Co., 1968), articles by Oscar Grusky, "Role Conflict in Organization: A Study of Prison Camp Officials" pp. 455-456. and Mayer N. Zald, "Power Balance and Staff Conflict in Correctional Institutions" pp. 397-425.

7. Gerber and McAnany, Contempora·y Punishment, Chapter 2, Retribution pp. 39-92.

8.   Confidential source.   Leading administration official in Rockefeller's administration.   Albany, March 1975.

9.   Barbara A. Lavin - participant observer.

10.   Interview with Vito Ternullo, former Director of the Division of Education in the Department of Correction.   Elmira, May 9, 1974.

11.   Interview with State Senator John R. Dunne, former Chairman of the New York State Senate Standing Committee on Penal Institutions, later changed to Committee on Crime and Corrections, Albany, March 17, 1975.

12.   Manual for the Use of the Legislature of the State of New York by John P. Lomenzo, Secretary of State, 1970, p. 630.

13.   Correctional policy in New York State is most evident in the custodial and treatment programs in the maximum security prisons for adult males.   These five prison institutions contained the largest number of incarcerated offenders in the state, and those offenders incarcerated for the most serious offenses.   By contrast, there was only one medium security prison for adult males, Wallkill, containing less than 5% of the total male prison population, in 1959.

14.   New York State Executive Budget.   Correction Department State Purposes Budget 1959-1960, pp. 151-170.   Rehabilitative positions included the following: Teacher, Vocational Instructor, Chaplain, Guidance Counselor.   (Toward the end of the 1960s, this basic rehabilitative staff was augumented by the positions of Psychiatrist and Psychologist.

15.   New York State Executive Budget.   Department of Correction.   State Purposes Budget, 1959-1960, pp. 151-170.

16.   New York State Executive Budget.   Department of Correction.   State Purposes Budget, 1957-1958, p. 167.

17.   New York State Executive Budget.   Department of Correction.   State Purposes Budget, 1959-1960, pp. 170-171.

18.   New York State Executive Budget.   Department of Correction.   State Purposes Budget, 1960-1961, p. 198.

19.   New York State Executive Budget.   Department of Correction.   State Purposes Budget, 1966-1967, p. 299.

20.   Ibid.

21. New York State Legislative Annual, p. 358. The Supreme Court decision in Baxstrom v. Herold 383 US 107 (February 21, 1966) had ruled that it was the responsibility of the state to provide suitable care for the criminally insane at the expiration of their prison sentence. New York State responded by establishing the State Beacon Institute for Defective Delinquents.
     For further information on the treatment of the criminally insane as it relates to court decisions see: Specht v. Patterson 87 S. Ct. 1209 (1967); U.S. v. Maroney 355 F2d 302 (3rd cir. 1966).
     The entire issue of insanity and criminality is now under review in the 1980s. For an interesting discussion of these issues see: Willard Gaylin, M.D. The Killing of Bonnie Garland (New York: Penguin Books, 1982).

22. Wardens and ultimately the Commissioner predicated their budgetary needs for the coming year on an estimated "projected" population. Therefore an increase in the "projected" population meant additional custody positions, a decreasing "projected" population meant loss of personnel positions. However, in projecting prison population for the years 1960-1963, the Department's estimate was lower than the actual count. See Correction - Executive Budget, State Purposes section for these years for itemized population count.

23. New York State Executive Budget. Department of Correction. State Purposes Budget 1963-1964, p. 736.

24. Interview with Vito Ternullo, May 9, 1974.

25. Interviews with: Frances Kernohan, Community Service Society. March 3, 1975; Austin MacCormick, Osborne Association, May 2, 1974; Gladys Burleigh and Don McEvoy, National Conference of Christians and Jews, March 1975.

26. Interview with Charles McKendrick, former Warden of Wallkill Prison, December 17, 1968.

27. American Friends Service Committee, Struggle for Justice (New York: Hill and Wang, 1971) p. 172.

28. New York State Executive Budget. Department of Correction. Capital Construction Budget 1966-1967, p. 812.

29. Interview with John R. Dunne, March 17, 1975.

30. Ibid.

31. Barbara A. Lavin - Participant Observer

32.   Interviews with Frances Kernohan, Community Service Society, March 3, 1975; Austin MacCormick, Osborne Association, May 2, 1974; Gladys Burleigh, National Conference of Christians and Jews, March 1975.

33.   Interview with Frances Kernohan, Community Service Society, March 3, 1975.

34.   Note: Original Correction Department Budgets are confidential documents. Therefore, the only empirical fiscal information available to researchers is the final Correction Department Budget as presented in the Governor's Executive Budget. Throughout this paper all correctional budgetary data was derived from the Governor's Executive Budget which will henceforth be referred to as: Correction - Executive Budget.

35.   H.H. Gerth and C. Wright Mills, From Max Weber: Essays in Sociology (New York: Oxford University Press, 1946) Chapter 8, "Bureaucracy" pp. 196-244.

36.   Interview with Vito Ternullo, May 9, 1974.

37.   Gerth and Mills, From Max Weber, Chapter 8, pp. 196-244.

38.   Note: Originally, the line item format was used in preparing the budget. Thus, information concerning the ratio of rehabilitative staff to custodial staff was readily discernible, since all personnel positions were listed for the various institutions. However, in the early 1960s gradual changes occurred in the budget format. The line item format was amended in favor of a program budget format. "Personnel Service" became a lump sum item which included all personnel in each of the institutions. No longer were the number of correction officers or rehabilitative staff enumerated in the budgets of the individual prisons. While new staff positions and the prison to which they were assigned were noted, it nevertheless became impossible, due to death and attrition, to determine the actual proportion of money spent for security versus rehabilitation programs - except insofar as new positions were allocated to the male prisons. Since the population breakdown of the individual prisons was not recorded consistently, it was no longer possible to determine if the allocation of additional correction officers to a particular prison reflected an actual increase in the prison population or additional security for the present inmate population.

It is interesting to note that the costs for maintenance and operation of the individual prisons continued to be represented on a line item budget.

Budgetary format was further amended in 1969-1970 and

program and personnel allocations for all of the male prisons were lumped under the general headings of "Care and Custody of Inmates" and "Rehabilitation of Offenders". As time progressed, it thus became more difficult to determine with any exactitude the ratio of rehabilitative staff to custodial staff. Only new positions were recorded and cumulative personnel information was omitted.

Most obervers contend that the changes in the budgetary format were the result of a need for flexibility and expediency and not a deliberate obfuscation of fact. It has been noted by David Roos, member of the Senate Minority Finance staff, in an interview in Albany on October 23, 1974, that the line item budgets provided no flexibility and that the change from line item budgets to program budget format was simply a matter of budget reform.

39.   Connery and Benjamin, Rockefeller of New York, pp. 118-120.

40.   Manual for the Use of the Legislature of the State of New York, Lomenzo, p. 478.

41.   As quoted in Connery and Benjamin, Rockefeller of New York, p. 119.

42.   Interview with John Corrigan, Administrator in charge of Correction Department Budget, Division of the Budget, March 21, 1975.

43.   Ibid. See also: Murray Edelman, Symbolic Uses of Politics. (Chicago: University of Illinois Press, 1967) pp. 22-72, on the symbolic responses inherent in a process which promotes personnel changes between an agency and a regulatory body.

44.   Interview with John Corrigan, March 21, 1975.

45.   Ibid.

46.   Confidential source. Leading administration official in Rockefeller's administration. Albany, March 1975.

47.   Interview with Vito Ternullo, May 9, 1974.

48.   Interview with John Corrigan, March 21, 1975.

49.   Ibid.

50.   Interview with Walter Dunbar, former New York State Deputy Commissioner of the Department of Correctional Services, May 29, 1974.
       Note: Name of Department changed from Department of

Correction to Department of Correctional Services when reorganizational schema went into effect in January 1970.

51.   Interview with Vito Ternullo, May 9, 1974.

52.   Interview with John Corrigan, March 21, 1975.

53.   Interview with John R. Dunne, March 17, 1975.

54.   Interview with Frances Kernohan, Community Service Society, March 3, 1975; Austin MacCormick, Osborne Association, May 2, 1974; Polly Feingold, Urban Coalition, May 1974.

55.   Interview with Russell G. Oswald, March 19, 1975.

56.   Interview with John R. Dunne, March 17, 1975.

57.   Legislative aide to upstate Republican Senator, March 1969.

58.   Barbara A. Lavin - Participant Observer.

59.   Interview with Charles McKendrick, December 17, 1968.

60.   Ibid.

61.   Gerald Benjamin, "Patterns in New York State Politics" in Governing New York State: The Rockefeller Years, Edited by Robert Connery and Gerald Benjamin (New York: The Academy of Political Science, May 1974) p. 31.

62.   Ibid.

63.   Ibid., p. 34-35.

64.   Stuart Witt, "Modernization of the Legislature" in Connery and Benjamin, Eds. Governing New York State: The Rockefeller Years, pp. 52-53.

65.   Benjamin, "Patterns in New York State Politics", p. 35.

66.   Robert Connery, "Nelson A. Rockefeller as Governor" in Connery and Benjamin, Eds., Governing New York State: The Rockefeller Years, p. 11.

67.   Interview with Vito Ternullo, May 9, 1974.

68.   Interview with John R. Dunne, March 17, 1975.

69.   Interview with Russell G. Oswald, March 19, 1975.

70. Interview with Frances Kernohan, March 3, 1975.

71. Interview with Matthew Fitzgerald, former New York State Director of the National Council on Crime and Delinquency, March 20, 1975.

72. Interviews with Don McEvoy and Gladys Burleigh, National Conference of Christians and Jews, March 1975.

73. Barbara A. Lavin - Participant Observer

74. New York Times, 25 March 1973, p. 47.

CHAPTER III

THE WIDENING OF THE CORRECTIONAL ARENA:

LEGISLATIVE INVOLVEMENT 1965-1970

Introduction

In this chapter, we will examine the major events in the broader arena of crime control legislation and policy in order to examine the role the Governor played in this arena and the effectiveness of the correctional bureaucracy vis-a-vis their opponents, where the wider arena overlapped their specific interests. In general, these events were indirectly supportive of correctional bureaucratic interests. Where this is so, there is little evidence of direct involvement by the correctional bureaucracy. This non-involvement of the correctional bureaucracy in this more visible arena was traditional, since it preferred to operate by direct communication of its Commissioner, McGinnis, to the Governor. (1) However, an analysis of this wider arena sets the stage for subsequent involvement of the correctional bureaucracy. Thus, a preliminary discussion of the following events is in order: Penal Law Revision, Governor Rockefeller's Law and Order Program, and the institution of the Narcotic Addiction Control Commission.

In the previous chapter, it was stated that the correctional bureaucracy was the recipient of tangible benefits through government's unfailing commitment to the status quo. It may also be remembered that, due to various judicial decisions which mandated the release of certain groups of criminal defectives(2) and improved parole services which allegedly resulted in fewer parole violators being returned to prison,(3) the state correctional system was faced with a declining state prison population (See Table 2. Note: to facilitate reading clarity, a distinction must be noted between state and city prison populations. One may increase, while the other decreases.) This situation was becoming increasingly acute during the late 1960s and the correctional bureaucracy was confronted with the possibility of loss of job positions. However, events in the broader arena of crime control will indicate how the bureaucracy was able to retain job security.

While still another interest group, the Black and Puerto Rican minorities, entered the correctional arena during the late 1960s, they were more or less quiescent and disorganized until the 1970s. Thus the activities of this group and its alliance with the reformers will not be discussed until Chapter four.

Penal Law Revision

In 1965, the Penal Law was revised for the first time since its enactment in 1881. Lawyers, and even judges, had been writing for some time about its structural disorganization(4) and internal inconsistencies and the revision was primarily concerned with these. (5) Historically, laws had been made as specific crimes demanded attention, thus there was no legal structural organization. Criminal sentences were mutually inconsistent. The revised Penal Law reduced all crimes to a few specific categories of gravity, each category having its proportionate sentence. (6) In accordance with the Neo-Classicist tradition, these sentences had a fixed minimum and maximum duration in order to deal with both the requirements of the crime itself, and with the personal requirements of the individual offender. The revision also provided for the possibility of probation in a wider range of crimes. (7)

There are several possible reasons for these changes in the penal code, none of which is specifically discussed in the literature. However, one can speculate that a general dissatisfaction with high recidivism rates indicating that prison was not working as a rehabilitative measure, and the fact that white middle class youths were being incarcerated on drug charges, all probably influenced decisions in the revised penal code regarding greater use of community treatment, that is, of probation.

These changes were not necessarily in the direct interests of the correctional bureaucracy since probation meant treatment in the community instead of incarceration in prison. However, the indeterminate sentence meant that the period to be served in the correctional institution was, in effect, set by the Parole Board, not by the judge (although the judge could, in appropriate cases, fix a minimum not to exceed one-third of the maximum). (8) While the Parole Board members were not members of the correctional bureaucracy, since appointed by the Governor, nevertheless the Parole Board's decisions, for all practical purposes, were based on the reports of the prison administration and the parole case worker assigned to the prison. (9) The decisions thus made were not subject to review by any power source outside the correction or parole bureaucracy. Thus indeterminate sentencing enabled the correctional bureaucracy to determine the population of the prison and simultaneously increased its control over the inmates through threat of non-parole.

It must be remembered that changes in the Penal Law came at a time of soaring crime rates, urban riots, backlogs in the judicial processing of criminal offenders and overcrowded conditions in the New York City prison and detention

44

facilities.(10)   (City jails usually held those convicted inmates whose sentence was less than one year as well as those accused offenders awaiting trial.)   These factors will be discussed in greater detail later on, but suffice it for now to indicate how the increased use of probation could relieve overcrowded conditions in city penal institutions and thus satisfy the demands of the New York City correctional bureaucracy for a manageable prison population when fiscal crises did not permit the hiring of additional correctional custodial staff.

Another datum relevant to our discussion is the fact that the mid-1960s was a period of increasing violence in America, especially in urban areas.   Racial tensions were high, precipitated, according to columnist Tom Wicker, by the

> unwelcome new insistence of Blacks,
> whether by non-violence or "black power"
> for a due share of jobs and affluence and
> an equal opportunity or more in schools,
> unions, political parties and the like.
> Opposing this was the determination of
> the just risen ethnics not to lose to black
> aspirants, the economic security and
> social status they had won by great
> effort.(11)

In New York, crime rates were soaring and fear of the criminal element was rampant among all classes.(12)   The public generally perceived the panacea to be a return to "law and order", believing that this could best be achieved by the traditional methods of law enforcement on the streets and harsh prison sentences intended as a deterrent.   They had little faith in the possibilities of social reforms in the communities or of rehabilitative policies in prisons and jails.(13)   Thus, increasingly, dragnet arrests, sidewalk shootouts, strong-arm tactics of all kinds and punitive prison terms were all justified in the attempt to preserve the status quo.(14)

Gerald Benjamin, political essayist of the Rockefeller years, has noted that the Governor had a predilection for public opinion polls.(15)   According to Benjamin, the Governor's ability to make major inroads in areas of normally overwhelming Democratic strength was due to his ability to gauge the concerns of the state's white ethnic population, as evidenced in the public opinion polls.(16)   In February of 1967, a New York Times article reported the findings of a recent Gallup poll which indicated that "for the first time since. . . the mid 1930s, crime and lawlessness are viewed by the public as the top domestic problem facing the nation."(17)   The article continued, "next to Vietnam, this is the issue that most certainly will have a powerful influence on the vote in November."(18) This popular conception of the problem gave rise to a sudden spurt of political interest in the criminal justice arena in the years 1966-1970.

Governor's Law and Order Program

Thus, Governor Nelson A. Rockefeller responded vigorously to the crime problem. A politician, to maintain the support of his constituency, must at least appear to be responsive to the concerns of that constituency. An examination of the Governor's actions in reference to the law and order problem shows they were in harmony with the interests of the correctional bureaucracy and the law enforcement interests generally. This, however, does not imply that the Governor responded solely to law enforcement interests. When law enforcement interests appeared to dominate the public scene, he manifested himself totally in favor of law enforcement. As other issues appeared, demanding different approaches, he manifested amenity to alternative or structurally innovative solutions, as will be shown later in this chapter.

On January 6, 1965, the Governor announced a major "anti crime" program in his Executive Message to the Legislature. At that time Rockefeller stated,

> major crime continues to increase at an alarming national rate of five times the growth in population. In New York State, the administration of criminal justice costs the state and its localities $665 million a year. Serious crimes - murder, rape, robbery, for example, have increased steadily since World War II. Brutal and shocking assaults are reported daily by our news media. And, most disheartening of all, youthful criminality has increased steadily. . . . Accordingly, I recommend the following Anti-Crime Program. . . . (19)

The essence of the program was greater law enforcement through use of increased police manpower.(20) Interest in the crime problem gave birth to subsequent conferences in 1966 and 1967. Both conferences were held in New York City and stressed the gravity of the crime problem while proposing law enforcement as its prime solution.

Police interests were well represented at both conferences as was the general public. Participants included: the American

46

Legion, New York State Association of Chiefs of Police, New York State Federation of Women's Clubs, Police Conference of New York, American Mothers, Inc., New York City Auxiliary Police and the New York State Council of Churches, among others. It should also be noted that the Governor was extremely visible at both conferences, speaking at the opening sessions, attending the various workshops, and mingling with the participants, his constituents.

Reform interests were minimally involved at the conferences. At the 1966 conference, reformers were only present on one panel out of the total of seven, a session entitled, "Citizen Involvement in the Administration of Criminal Justice."(21) At the 1967 conference, there was no reform group representation on any of the panels.(22) Law enforcement interests thus dominated both conferences.

For example, at the 1967 conference, Louis Lefkowitz, Attorney General of New York State, spoke of the damage to the business interests of the city while noting the effect of rising crime rates and public fear of crime on the economy of the city. He alluded to: a declining tourist trade, the difficulties a major university was having recruiting faculty, and pressure from the hotel workers union specifically, all the result of the increased incidence of crime in the streets. Lefkowitz stated,

> May I say that as far as I am concerned, the immediate question is how can you police the streets more effectively to eliminate, as far as possible this growing fear. . . . The immediate problem as far as I am concerned is extra police on the beat.(23)

And extra police on the streets would ultimately result in more arrests and greater use of incarceration.

The Governor's Program was a response to these demands: expansion of the State Police by five hundred additional positions; plans for the consolidation of some six hundred separate police departments in the state into larger, more effective units;(24) a minimum salary for local police; full time District Attorneys in large counties; clear legal authority for wire tapping and electronic surveillance; and stricter firearms control.(25) In the previous year, 1966, a computerized system for the efficient tracking and identifying of former felons had been established at the recommendation of the Governor.(26)

Once again, there is no evidence of direct involvement by the correctional bureaucracy in these decisions, but these

47

decisions were in no way deleterious to their interests. In fact, these decisions would be advantageous to their interests since increased arrests would generally result in increased prison clientele.

Narcotic Addiction Control Commission (NACC)

During this same period, the rising crime rates came to be viewed as a direct result of an increased level of narcotic addiction. In 1966, in a special message to the Legislature, the Governor had stated,

> addiction spreads through a neighborhood like a virulent infection. Its unfortunate victims, prisoners of a relentless craving, lure the weak into the habit in order to help obtain drugs for themselves. With this infection comes crime - theft, burglary, mugging, prostitution, assault and murder.(27)

Addiction and crime were always asserted as a cause/effect relationship, and this assertion could help the correctional bureaucracy to achieve its own ends. The following discussion of Governor Rockefeller's drug control program, the Narcotic Addiction Control Commission, will demonstrate how the Narcotic Addiction Control Commission (NACC) was a tangible response to the broader law enforcement interests.

Alan Chartock, in his article titled, "Narcotic Addiction: the Politics of Frustration", has noted that "most of the major political initiatives in the area of drug abuse control in New York over the past decade were taken by Governor Nelson A. Rockefeller".(28) Chartock continued,

> in February of 1966, approximately eight months before he ran for his third term, Rockefeller announced an all out war on drugs and addiction. Knowing his electorate well, he was fully aware of their frustration and fear. Polls had told him that crime and addiction were two of his constituents' greatest fears. . . . (29)

One aspect of the Governor's drug program was especially geared to public concern for action against drug dealers, namely more severe penalties for pushers. According to Chartock, "this was nothing new; New York politicians had long realized that stiffer penalties for pushers was a safe political position".(30)

New laws had been enacted in 1965 which attempted to regulate the possession and sale of narcotic medicines such as amphetamines, barbiturates and hallucinogenic drugs and also to control the sale of prescriptions for narcotic medicines to minors.(31)   In 1966, the Governor recommended more severe prison sentences for those convicted of sale of narcotics, especially to minors.(32)   Limited bail rights were accorded those suspected of narcotic involvement either as "pushers" or addicts.(33)   In 1967, the Legislature defined LSD and depressant or stimulant drugs as dangerous drugs, the sale of which could be subject to penalties of up to twenty-five years imprisonment.(34)   These harsher prison terms were also in the interests of the bureaucracy for it would make their jobs more secure by mandating incarceration instead of some other form of punishment.   However, it was in the form of the treatment program for addicts (NACC) that the bureaucracy received its most immediate expression of governmental support.

As the addiction problem became more acute and the public increasingly concerned with rising crime rates which they associated with addiction, the Governor inaugurated his own treatment program entitled, the Narcotic Addiction Control Commission (NACC).   According to one observer, New York State, during Rockefeller's administration, poured more money and effort into the treatment of illegal drug users than any other jurisdiction in the country.(35)   In administration and direction, NACC was harmonious with the correctional bureaucratic interests as well as the law and order interests of the Governor's constituency, for NACC was a treatment program with a strong incarceration component.(36)

. According to Chartock,

> there was little recorded opposition in the final vote in the legislature on the 1966 Drug Bill.   Democrats and Republicans alike were frightened by constituent perceptions of them as voting against a narcotic solution. . . . The final vote in the Senate was 57-4 and the vote in the Assembly was an equally lopsided 151-8.(37)

NACC was thus established as an autonomous body under the aegis of the Department of Mental Hygiene and provided for the establishment of treatment facilities for those youth certified as addicts.

Addicts could be certified to NACC in three ways: 1) civil certification of addicts not accused or convicted of crime, via a court order, 2) commitment of convicted narcotic addicts and 3) civil commitment after arrest but before trial. (38)   In two of the three instances, addicts were certified for treatment without an actual criminal conviction.   These addicts thus certified could be treated in community residential facilities and diverted away from direct involvement in the criminal justice system. (39)   But certification as an addict always resulted in some form of compulsory treatment and confinement whether in a NACC operated community based residential facility or in a correctional facility, i.e., the prisons and jails.   In the 1968-1969 fiscal year, over six hundred narcotic addicts were accepted for "treatment and supervision" in the state correctional facilities. (40)   And in this latter case, NACC is important for the light it sheds on the de facto support given to the correctional bureaucratic interests.

Under NACC, various treatment modalities were funded and many of these were run by private agencies.   Punitive incarceration had long been criticized as being ineffective in curing drug use problems. (41) The policies espoused by NACC, namely, therapy and rehabilitation, would seem by their very nature to be antithetical to the historical conditions of the prisons, and as such, should have been threatening to the correctional bureaucracy which was merely custody oriented. Nevertheless, the correctional bureaucracy did receive benefits under the new programs.   Several correctional facilities, namely Woodbourne Correctional Institution and sections of Albion State Training School, Matteawan State Hospital and Green Haven Prison were "temporarily" transferred to NACC for use as treatment facilities.   Personnel positions were also transferred from the Correction Department budget to the NACC budget.   Guards who formerly worked for the Correction Department retained their jobs and seniority, but now technically worked for NACC. (42)   Thus, the correctional bureaucracy suffered no lay-offs or dismissals despite the declining prison population.   As noted in the 1969-1970 Correction - Executive Budget, funds for the treatment and custody of the certified addicts in these correctional facilities were provided by NACC. (43)

Thus, the Governor's drug program and inauguration of NACC may in part be viewed as a tangible expression of support to the correctional bureaucracy who were thereby able to retain their jobs and seniority.

It is difficult to document the activities by which the correctional bureaucracy achieved these benefits, since there is no obvious record of its activity.   However, it was common knowledge in the field at that time that the correctional bureaucracy operated through their Commissioner, McGinnis, who made their needs known to his friend and supporter, Lieutenant Governor Malcolm Wilson. (44)

Of course, one could also assert that an established bureaucracy need not actively politic to exercise influence since habitually we have always taken an existing bureaucracy to be the solver of the particular problem it has always dealt with, even when the theoretical method of solving the problem has completely changed. In other words, it achieves benefits because it is there.

Or one could make a logical argument for the fact of active use of influence by the correctional bureaucracy. As noted before, the NACC treatment model was antithetical to that of the traditional correctional bureaucracy and as such should not have afforded benefits to it. The very fact that it did afford these benefits would suggest the active use of influence to bring about this illogical "association".

Despite the weaknesses of merely inferential arguments, we can assert that in these three instances, the revision of the Penal Law, the Governor's Law and Order Program, and the inauguration of NACC, the correctional bureaucracy had received tangible benefits insofar as these programs increased the potential pool of prisoners in state correctional facilities.

Governor's Special Committee on Criminal Offenders

During this same time period, the correctional bureaucracy perceived a more serious threat to their interests in the form of a gubernatorial committee, the Governor's Special Committee on Criminal Offenders, which had been established in 1966, to study the criminal justice system in New York State. According to Rockefeller, the purpose of the committee was to find ways of rehabilitating first offenders, propose improved methods of dealing with convicted criminal offenders, evaluate treatment concepts and analyze current correctional services.(45) An appropriation of $200,000 was made for the work of the Committee.

The members of the Committee, the Commissioners of Correction, Parole, Social Services, Narcotic Addiction Control Commission, Mental Hygiene, Division for Youth, and the State Administrator of the Judicial Conference, were the voices of the bureaucracy; in many cases, these Commissioners had come "up from the ranks" and thus were insiders. However, the working staff of the Committee was not of the bureaucracy and did not represent their interests. The working staff of the Committee was predominantly composed of lawyers. The executive director was Peter Preiser, attorney and Westchester Republican. According to one observer, Preiser, who had been appointed by Rockefeller, had little prior knowledge of the correctional system in New York State.(46)

51

According to the Preliminary Report of the Committee, issued in June 1968, the original proposals had been suggested by the members of the committee, namely the Commissioners or their representatives. "The action projects were to deal with legislative proposals and governmental pilot programs involving steps that the members - through their experience in disciplines dealing with the post adjudicatory aspects of crime and delinquency - believed should be taken as soon as possible."(47) One such legislative proposal was signed into law in 1966 and authorized the Board of Parole to issue certificates to first offenders which would preserve or restore the right to vote and would remove mandatory bars to the right to apply for licenses and other privileges. Known as the "Certificate of Relief from Disabilities", the certificate, issued by the court or Parole Board after the ex-offender had spent five crime-free years in the community, provided access to jobs requiring licenses such as barbering, cosmetology and others.(48) In theory, the reformers supported the rehabilitative thrust of such a measure, although there is no indication that this bill originated with them or was in response to their demands.(49)

Several other proposals in the mental health mode of rehabilitation were set forth by the Governor's Special Committee. The Clinton Diagnostic and Treatment Center established during fiscal year 1967- 1968 was to provide intensive treatment and special casework services for psychotic inmates to prepare them for release on parole. The Center was to utilize the therapeutic community approach in an attempt to get the inmates to behave in a manner as "close as possible to free behavior in the community."(50) The number of inmates served however was minimal and the project was to encounter funding problems in the following years. As such, the Center could hardly be considered more than an experimental model.

Other measures, stemming from federal court action concerning the rights and confinement of the criminally insane,(51) were implemented as committee recommendations. Beacon State Institution was established for the care of defective delinquents and a new institution was recommended for mentally retarded offenders. These institutions were under the control of the correctional bureaucracy and employed bureaucratic personnel whose roles had merely been widened. The law permitting indefinite life sentences for mental defectives was eliminated and mental defectives were accorded the same right to good behavior allowances granted other inmates. A Special Sociopath Research Experiment was initiated for persistent psychopathic offenders, utilizing medication, the use of mild electric shock, and chemotherapy.

It is interesting to note that such proposals, acceded to by the Governor, Nelson A. Rockefeller, might appear to be diametrically opposed to the "law and order" stance previously espoused by him. However, as Connery and Benjamin have noted,

> pragmatists are result oriented. They need not be consistent, either across or within policy areas. Inconsistency across policy may easily be explained as an effort to make the best decision in a particular case. . . . The very flexibility inherent in the problem-solving approach makes it exceedingly difficult to pin down the executive for an evaluative analysis.(52)

Thus, where new programs were initiated, they were very much in the mental health mode of rehabilitative services; although reform involvement in these proposals cannot be documented. However, since the structure of the bureaucracies was unchanged, the programs discussed above can best be characterized as either appendages or experimental models that could be disposed of or discontinued at will, leaving bureaucratic structures intact.

One year after the specific action grant programs described above were formulated, the focus of the committee shifted dramatically to "an indepth evaluation of a program to coordinate and combine all of the state's efforts concerned with the treatment and rehabilitation of criminal offenders, including the consolidation of all of the state's institutional programs and field services in this area."(53) Governor Nelson A. Rockefeller directed the Special Committee on Criminal Offenders to report its findings in the early part of 1968. The focus of the committee had thus changed greatly from individual programs to major structural reorganization and consolidation of services and this change of focus threatened the existence of the separate, already established bureaucracies.

Several factors appear to have influenced this shift in emphasis. For example, there is some evidence that a similar commission with similar objectives had been set up in 1959 and headed by William Ronan, Special Assistant and confidant of Nelson A. Rockefeller.(54) Although no public records of this earlier commission can be located, Robert Connery in his article, "Nelson A. Rockefeller as Governor", alludes to Ronan's influence in presenting administrative reorganization proposals to the Governor.(55) However, Connery also notes that,

> although the Governor supported these

plans to provide for a more symmetrical
structure, few of them were accepted by
the Legislature. In Rockefeller's later
years as Governor, he was more inclined
to use reorganization as a means of
infusing fresh leadership into programs in
which he was interested, and he was not
as concerned about theoretical
considerations. (56)

It has also been asserted that the shift in direction toward
structural reorganization was the brain child of Peter Preiser and
his staff of lawyers. According to the Assistant Director of the
Committee, John Delaney,

the reorganization proposal was the brain
child of the lawyers on the staff of the
Special Committee. As such, it was a
status quo conservative reformulation of
the problem. . . . Lawyers, because of
their discipline, are predisposed to
consider organizational solutions, to look
at legal structures and not theoretical
issues. (57)

Other factors, no doubt, had as prevailing an influence.
There was, at this time, increasing pressure on the state
correctional system from county and city (especially New York
City) correctional systems. By law, every county was mandated
to maintain a county jail and to house both offenders awaiting
disposition of cases and those whose sentences were less than one
year. Also, state prisoners were remanded to city facilities for
court appearances as parole violators or coram nobis prisoners.
The rising crime rates which had meant increased arrests and
overcrowded detention facilities had resulted in a high tax burden
for local jurisdictions which had to pay the costs of housing the
offenders or suspected offenders as well as the costs for
maintenance and renovation of these facilities. Consequently,
there was increasing pressure on the State Department of
Correction to assume all costs relating to the care of those
offenders, technically state prisoners, serving terms of less than
one year.

As John R. Dunne, Chairman of the New York State Senate
Committee on Penal Institutions, had noted in his 1967 legislative
report, the majority of the bills referred to his Committee in the
1967 session had dealt with a demand for state financial assistance
for local correctional services. (58) Pressure was especially
intense from the New York City correctional system,
overburdened with an increasing jail population, outmoded

facilities and severe overcrowding. It had been estimated in December of 1966 that the actual cost of housing state prisoners in the New York City facilities was more than double the five dollars per day per capita cost then provided by the state.(59)

Several bills had been introduced during the 1967 legislative session which would have lifted the ceiling on state reimbursement for state prisoners located in New York City jails. The reform groups, and especially the Youth and Correction Committee of the Community Service Society, wholeheartedly supported full state reimbursement to local institutions for the housing of state prisoners.

> We can see no rhyme or reason to the present requirement that only a portion of these costs be borne by the state. . . . We believe that the state should assume full responsibility for the costs of maintaining its prisoners regardless of the institutions in which they are housed.(60)

Nevertheless, despite reform support, all of the bills dealing with state reimbursement of local correctional facilities either died or were defeated in Committee - in the Penal Institutions Committee of which Dunne was Chairman, or in the Finance Committee.

However, the greatest threat to the correctional bureaucracy was in the final and most extensive recommendation of the Governor's Special Committee, namely, the entire reorganization of correctional services in New York State through direct state administration of all services for individuals adjudicated on the basis of "anti-social" behavior. This would have achieved what the reformers and the New York City Correctional Administration could not achieve via the legislative arena.

Thus, a unified treatment agency was proposed, namely, The Department of Rehabilitative Services (DRS) which would unite the functions of the Department of Correction, Division of Parole, Probation, Narcotic Addiction Control Commission, Division for Youth and the Division of Social Services into one agency. Thus the state would directly administer all custodial treatment of convicted offenders including sentenced offenders in county jails and penitentiaries, as well as all pre-sentence and pre-disposition reporting functions of the Probation and Court systems. Three separate units within the DRS would be established based on maturity levels; one for children, one for youth and one for adults with provision for transfer between levels.

Thus the scope of the DRS, as envisioned by the

Governor's Special Committee, was extensive and if implemented, would have resulted in a powerful unified superstructure in the criminal justice arena. Since the state would have assumed total responsibility for all sentenced prisoners as well as those awaiting disposition of case, New York City and other local correctional systems would have been relieved of problems concerning overcrowded facilities and fiscal indebtedness.

In fact, enabling legislation was never drafted due to vociferous opposition by the bureaucracies involved, that is, Corrections, Parole, Social Services, Narcotic Addiction Control Commission and the Division for Youth. Individually they would have lost job positions, program monies and, especially, power and autonomy. Commissioner of Social Services, George Wyman, wrote a lengthy disavowal of the Committee's recommendations for a unified treatment agency.(61) Paul McGinnis and others apparently agreed with Wyman. McGinnis has stated,

> there were several things in the
> Governor's Special Committee Report that
> I did not agree with and I know that
> there were a lot of other people who sat
> around that table who shared my
> opinion.(62)

Moreover, McGinnis was not merely opposed to the theoretical concept of a unified treatment agency, but was opposed to any housing of New York City inmates in state institutions. New York City inmates, most from minority backgrounds, increasingly had a reputation as troublemakers and radicals.(63) And McGinnis, interested primarily in security and the status quo, was not likely to approve any measure which might upset the custodial balance of power between guards and inmates. Despite the "underpopulated" state prison system, McGinnis did not want New York City inmates, and he had already been forced to make several concessions in this matter.

Two years previously, in 1966, pressure from the New York City Correctional administration and the Office of the Mayor had mandated legislative changes which had forced McGinnis to accept some city prisoners. Chapter 650 of the Correction Laws of 1966 had provided, "emergency assistance to New York City to relieve severe overcrowding in the House of Detention for Women and other New York City detention facilities." This bill, submitted at the request of the Governor, authorized the Commissioner of Correction to establish a State Detention Facility, which could have included portions of existing state correctional institutions, to house city prisoners. Chapter 651 of the Correction Laws of 1966 had authorized the State Commissioner of Correction to lease to any city or county a part of any state facility under the jurisdiction of the Commissioner of Correction to be used as an adjunct to a city or county jail or penitentiary for the confinement of females sentenced to such jails or penitentiaries. Later, males would be included.

According to George McGrath, New York City Commissioner of Correction,

> Mayor Lindsay had to force through this legislation under great opposition. . . . We first had to file a bill, Mayor Lindsay did, to permit the women to be transferred to the state. Then the following year, we amended it to permit males to be transferred. And then the matter of actually getting the transfer done, I think, was done with a lot of foot dragging. . . . In the end, the State Commissioner of Correction, McGinnis, agreed to a compromise solution, namely, to take up to a thousand inmates from New York City jails and prisons to relieve the overcrowding. (64)

More and more New York City prisoners were thus transferred to state institutions as far away as Auburn (near the city of Syracuse), Attica (near Buffalo), and Dannemora (near the Canadian border). Napanoch, a former reformatory in the Catskills, was devoted entirely to housing young Black and Puerto Rican inmates from New York City. (65)

But complete state take over of all New York City sentenced inmates was not effected by the legislation of 1966, nor by the recommendations of the Governor's Special Committee in 1968. Bureaucratic concern for the preservation of the status quo, without allegedly rebellious inmates, was too strong a countervailing force. The DRS was soundly defeated by bureaucratic interests before it was even drafted into a legislative proposal.

It is interesting to note that although the DRS would have been in part responsive to the reformers' advocacy of state take over of sentenced prisoners, according to the reformers' own admission, they were not formally or directly involved in the deliberations of the Governor's Special Committee regarding the formulation of the DRS. The following reform groups had testified at public hearings held by the Special Committee in 1966: Community Service Society, Correctional Association of New York, and the National Council on Crime and Delinquency. Their testimony supported specific treatment programs such as: work release and furlough programs (which permitted an inmate some contact with the community either for a job or for family contact), halfway houses, conjugal visits and the amplification of educational programs within the institutions.(66) However, the programs supported by the reformers bear little resemblance to the final report of the Special Committee.

The reformers themselves appear to have been apathetic concerning the final report of the Special Committee. As Frances Kernohan, former staff associate of the Community Service Society's Committee on Youth and Correction, has noted,

> we supported the DRS and the Special Committee Report in principle and we were one of the very few groups who did make any statement on it at all, even though we had no initial input into the report and were not asked to participate even in an advisory capacity. . . . But we supported the Final Report only in principle - by a telegram.(67)

The role of the National Council on Crime and Delinquency in the deliberation of the Governor's Special Committee is an enigma. NCCD, organized in 1907, is a quasi reform, quasi professional national organization comprised of approximately 60,000 citizens and crime control officials. In the criminal justice arena, NCCD is highly respected for its educational publications and citizen action programs.

NCCD had been formally asked by the Governor to serve as an advisory body to the Special Committee, and they did submit consultant reports as also did the American Correctional Association, a professional organization of correctional personnel, and the Cresap Consulting Firm. However, these reports were not publicized.(68) Insiders believe that the reports were not distributed because they were critical of and threatening to the correctional bureaucracy. One former Department of Correction official believed the reports were highly critical of security measures within the institutions.(69) Others believe the reports were critical of Parole.(70) And even though NCCD was serving as advisor to the Committee, the New York State Director of NCCD was not permitted to see the contents of the reports and was told by his superiors at national headquarters, "it is better that you do not know what is in the reports."(71)

The New York State Council of NCCD was rarely consulted by the Special Committee.(72) According to the former Director, Matthew Fitzgerald, "Preiser called us together only once in that two year period. . . reformers were never asked for ideas by the

58

administration. The Governor always sought the reports from professional agencies."(73)

The New York State Council of NCCD appears at best to have been nominally involved as a reform group in Committee deliberations. However, at the national level, NCCD may even have been supportive of bureaucratic interests; but, with the absence of the consultant reports, this remains conjecture.

Very little of the original proposal for the DRS was formulated into legislation. The Committee released its final report in 1968; enabling legislation which greatly modified the original proposal was formulated in 1969.

The final package of Governor's bills which resulted provided in part for the unification of the Department of Correction and the Division of Parole into a new Department of Correctional Services. The ramifications of this proposal which passed the legislature and was signed into law will be further developed in Chapter 4. Suffice it to mention now that, in theory, neither bureaucracy was to lose job positions nor "territorial integrity". The unification was to be nominal, only since both bureaucratic structures would remain intact and fulfill separate functions. They were to be united merely in name, with one Commissioner and to receive unified direction and policy. However, in practice, when Governor Nelson A. Rockefeller appointed the Commissioner of Parole, Russell G. Oswald as Commissioner of this new Department of Correctional Services in January of 1970, the correctional bureaucracy felt threatened since they perceived that Oswald did not share their custodial orientation.(74)

In addition, legislation provided that Probation be taken out of the Department of Correction and made a separate entity within the Executive Department. Other legislation changed the names of the facilities from "prisons" to "correctional facilities" and the titles from "wardens" to "superintendents", a purely symbolic change. A proposal advocating the establishment of regional facilities by merging several county jail populations into one regional facility was vetoed by the Legislature due to intensive lobbying efforts by the sheriffs of the state. Regional facilities would have meant a great loss of patronage for the county politicians who could influence the choices for sheriff, matron (usually the sheriff's wife) and the guards.

The Governor's Special Committee disbanded and regrouped in 1969 under the title of Crime Control Council. This was to be a permanent agency "to devote continuous attention to comprehensive planning in the prevention and control of crime, and to stimulate, develop and coordinate improved crime control programs throughout the state."(75)   The Council was envisioned as a means of cooperation between state and local forces in criminal justice and was also to carry on the work begun by the Governor's Special Committee on Criminal Offenders.   However, nothing significant came of this Council since, in 1969, attention in this area shifted from structural reorganization to administration of federal monies intended for community based programs, available through the Federal Safe Streets Act of 1968.

Legislative Arena

So far the data indicate that the reformers were not an effective force for change.   As late as October of 1969, reform groups were still urging a state take over of all sentenced prisoners in local institutions to relieve inhumane overcrowding and to provide for rehabilitative programming not fiscally viable in local institutions.(76)   But until this time, it appeared that no one was listening to their demands.   Their persistent role was one of "outsider".   Nevertheless, the reformers did appear to have a spokesman in the Chairman of the Senate Committee on Penal Institutions, John R. Dunne, and one of the measures the reformers supported in principle, work release programs, was enacted into law.

John R. Dunne, a junior member of the New York State Senate, had been appointed Chairman of the Penal Institutions Committee in 1966.   A Long Island Republican, from a solidly middle class district, Dunne had had no prior interest in corrections before the Committee assignment.(77)   Outside the pale of Republican power on Long Island and in the Senate as well, Dunne had been given the least attractive of all Committee assignments, but he resigned himself to "do what he could" with it.(78)   Extensive reading, visits to penal institutions and involvement with reformers and bureaucrats alike soon prepared Dunne to become a knowledgeable spokesman on correctional issues.   But even Dunne's involvement in correctional legislation was more that of "reactor" than "initiator".   A discussion of the innovative "Work Release" legislation will demonstrate this point.

Work release, although begun in Wisconsin in 1917, was an apparently new concept in New York State.   Such a program would permit a convicted prisoner, toward the end of his sentence, to be employed outside the prison institution during working hours and then return to the prison at night and on weekends to serve the remainder of his term.   The prisoner's wages would be placed in a trust account, and distributed according to a formula which gave a portion of the wages to his family for their support, a portion to the state to pay the cost of room and board while incarcerated, and a portion placed in a bank account to be given to the inmate upon his release from the institution.

In theory, work release was viewed as a humane, rehabilitative program, a means of bridging the gap between prison and society, between the inmate and his family. On a much more pragmatic level, it could serve to alleviate overcrowded prison conditions and to defray the expenses of the prison by having the inmate contribute to the costs of his or her incarceration. This was one issue that had broad reform support.

The 1967 Report of the Youth and Correction Committee of the Community Service Society on pending legislation, noted that "we strongly hold that work release programs are a valuable rehabilitative method which provides opportunities for involvement in the community as a preliminary step to parole or release."(79) Other reform groups such as the New York State Council of the National Council on Crime and Delinquency and the Correctional Association of New York also supported the work release legislation. However, despite reform support, such legislation was not released from Dunne's Committee. Dunne has stated,

> among other bills not discharged from Committee were some which anticipated proposals expected to be raised by the Governor's Special Committee on Criminal Offenders. Among these was SI 1584 (Warner) to establish a work release program for inmates of state correctional institutions. A similar bill AI 4305 (Thorpe) passed the Assembly but applied only to county jails. The Governor's Commission is scheduled to publish next year, findings and recommendations concerning the entire correctional system. (80)

And so, legislative consideration of work release was postponed, ostensibly to await the Governor's recommendations on the matter.

Connery, in his commentary on "Nelson A. Rockefeller as Governor", noted,

> Rockefeller working closely with the two majority leaders, usually had little difficulty in getting his programs through the legislature. What the legislature lacked, however, was the ability to develop new programs and this was the principal input of the Governor. Since

61

most programs originated in the
Governor's office, one might say that the
Governor proposed and the legislature
disposed.(81)

But work release legislation was not forthcoming in the
recommendations of the Governor's Special Committee, possibly
because Paul McGinnis, Commissioner of the Department of
Correction and member of the Governor's Special Committee, was
opposed to the idea. McGinnis had stated that the issue needed
further study and noted the vast array of rehabilitation and
vocational training programs then operating in the state system
and the difficulty in finding employment for prisoners in the
isolated communities which housed the state prison
institutions.(82) McGinnis was thus influential in delaying the
legislative mandate for work release programs in the state penal
institutions - but it was to be a delay of only two years.

Meanwhile, Senator Dunne had become a more visible
spokesman for reform measures. In 1968, he conducted a series
of hearings on the "Criminal Recidivist - Causes and Cures".
This set of 1968 public hearings, held in New York City and
Albany, discussed the issue of work release. The purpose of the
hearings, as stated by Dunne, was

to focus attention on the problem of the
criminal repeater, the recidivist, and
steps society must take to reverse this
trend in order to protect itself. Second,
the Senate Committee intends to develop
specific solutions to the problem.(83)

Many pieces of legislation were drafted or amended in
consultation with the Governor's Counsel or members of his legal
staff,(84) and the legislative proposal for work release no doubt
had the Governor's support. Legislation which authorized the
New York City Commissioner of Correction to inaugurate work
release programs in city institutions was subsequently introduced
by Dunne at the request of the Governor,(85) was passed, and
signed into law in 1968. The following year, work release
programs were authorized for the state correctional system, an
apparent tangible response to reform interests. However, even
work release legislation might be viewed as a token allocation of
benefits since in 1971, after three years, a total of only 108
prisoners had been accorded the benefits of work release(86) at a
time when the average population of the adult male prisons in the
state was 8,700 inmates. (See Table 2)

At this time, still another reform issue, that of prisoner
rights, was brewing in the institutions and further demands were

being made for less restrictions on reading material, visiting privileges and censorship of mail. The correctional bureaucracy was increasingly faced with rebellious Black and Puerto Rican inmates and did not know how to deal with the situation. It is symptomatic of this trouble that S 4900, a Rules bill, was introduced and signed into law by the Governor as Chapter 319 of the Correction Laws of 1969. This bill permitted the Commissioner of Correction to transfer inmates without restriction, something the correctional bureaucracy had been seeking as a way of isolating troublemakers.(87) According to Russell G. Oswald,

> at this time, protests were not usually well organized and the individual or individuals responsible were transferred to other state prisons. This constant system of transferals kept the prisons relatively quiet.(88)

In the Legislature, none of the bills concerning prisoner right to worship, clothing allowances, nor segregation of first offenders was acted upon and so "died" in the Penal Institutions Committee. The reformers had issued no statements of support. One such bill which would have increased the minimum clothing allowance from fifteen to thirty dollars for prisoners discharged from the county penitentiary if in summer, and from twenty-five to an increase of thirty dollars if in winter, was passed by the Legislature but vetoed by the Governor on jurisdictional grounds. During the 1969 legislative session, Assemblyman Hardt introduced a bill relating to religious freedom within the prisons. Hardt's memo noted that "at the present time the Department of Correction has a policy of not permitting baptism by immersion and during the past two years, on two occasions, I have had to intervene through the Governor's office to permit the baptism by immersion for the inmates." Hardt's bill authorizing baptism by immersion within the prisons was passed and signed into law. Thus, McGinnis' control of the institutions did not permit change through administrative channels but resulted in even minor changes having to be effected through legislative channels.

Consequently, this legislative involvement indicates a widening of the arena which was previously almost the sole purview of the correctional bureaucracy. Now, other factions were making their voices heard and achieving some change through the legislature.(89)

Yet other legislation which would have indicated a real strength of reform interests was not implemented. Senate bill S 3470, introduced in 1965, which would have authorized the State Commission of Correction, a regulatory agency, to promulgate rules and regulations establishing minimum standards for the care, custody, treatment, training, education, discipline, employment and other correctional programs for all persons confined in correctional institutions in New York City, with the power to close any failing to comply with such rules and regulations, was left on the Calendar at the close of the session. Even when enabling legislation was passed, often the money to implement the program was not authorized. For example, Chapter 655 of the Laws of 1966 authorized the Commissioner of Correction to establish community based residential facilities for state prisoners who would soon become eligible for parole. However, funds were not made available for this project. As Paul McGinnis had stated, "two years ago (1968) we got the legislation, but never got the money to set up the halfway house in New York City."(90) Note McGinnis' seeming support for the one program which would have resulted in the early release of New York City prisoners from state institutions.

It is interesting to note that the reformers themselves perceived their role to be "reactors to" instead of "initiators of" legislation. In the 1967 Legislative Report of the Community Service Society's Committee on Youth and Correction, it was noted that, "as usual, several important bills were introduced so late in the session as to make responsible analysis impossible. This practice inhibits debate and curtails worthwhile public reaction. . . . "(91)

In the absence of effective lobbying by reformers for institutional change, the correctional bureaucracy remained more or less secure in their maintenance of the status quo.

While at the end of 1970, rehabilitative positions, which were antithetical to the custodial orientation of the correctional bureaucracy and which demanded personnel composed of correctional bureaucratic "outsiders" had increased 100 percent, from 3 percent of the total prison staff in 1960 to 6 percent in 1970, yet custody-oriented personnel retained 73 percent of an increased total of the positions available. (See Table 3) Thus, in effect, the correctional bureaucracy had not lost positions.

Yet statements by McGinnis before the joint Senate Finance and Assembly Ways and Means Committee in February of 1968 shed further light on the allocation of resources to rehabilitation programs. McGinnis stated then,

> we have twenty-two vacancies in the
> Education program, including teachers
> and vocational instructors, out of a total
> of 329 positions. . . . In all of our
> prisons, the Education program is very
> light, but we are trying to strengthen

64

them.(92)

McGinnis continued,

> we have had to use correction officers as
> counselors because we do not have
> trained guidance counselors. . . .
> Corrections has the same problem year
> after year of trying to fill positions. We
> simply do not have the money."(93)

But while the inmates had remained quiescent until this point, they were not to do so for long. As Commissioner Russell G. Oswald has noted, in 1967, due to the passage of the Federal Civil Rights Act, corrections suits were now handled by federal courts instead of the more conservative state courts.

> Federal courts are traditionally far more
> liberal than state courts and so decisions
> were made supporting prisoner rights and
> reform measures. In those suits initiated
> on behalf of the inmates, the federal
> courts took the side of the inmates.(94)

The success attained by the inmates in federal court led to increased militancy and rebellion within prison walls.(95) This militancy would in 1970 burst forth in riots in New York City jails and later in 1971 in Attica State Prison.

It must also be noted that prior to the riots at the Tombs and Attica, the press (newspapers) was not involved in correctional issues in any way. According to Commissioner Oswald,

> the press was not involved primarily
> because the metropolitan news system of
> New York State was based in New York
> City and thus oriented to New York City
> news. The upstate prisons were not
> considered newsworthy. In addition, the
> correctional officers were not politically
> oriented insofar as they did not use the
> press as their public arena or inform the
> press as to trouble within the
> institutions. McGinnis exerted too strong
> a control for that to occur.(96)

The correctional officers and the Commissioner were interested in security, an enclosed system and keeping things quiet.

Thus, the correctional bureaucracy remained a vital force supportive of the status quo, despite: the revision of the Penal Law; the Governor's Law and Order Program; inauguration of NACC; the Governor's Special Committee on Criminal Offenders' proposal of the DRS with its effort to create a super-agency; legislative measures dealing with such as work release and the institution of the rehabilitative mode in corrections; and the beginnings of inmate demands. The reformers, in turn, received slight gains even though legislative decisions were not backed by adequate funding.

The year 1970 marked the ever increasing involvement of the fourth interest, relatively dormant since 1848, - the minority groups incarcerated within the prison system. Chapter four is primarily the story of their involvement in the correctional arena.

Endnotes - Chapter III

1. Interview with former Warden Charles L. McKendrick, Wallkill State Prison, December 1968.

2. Baxstrom v. Herold 383 US 107 (February 21, 1966)

3. New York State Correction - Executive Budget, 1966-1967, p. 299.

4. Marvin E. Frankel, Criminal Sentences (New York: Hill and Wang, 1972), Chapter 1, "Law Without Order or Limit", pp. 3-11.

5. Governor Nelson A. Rockefeller's Conference on Crime. Proceedings, April 21-22, 1966 p. 68. Statement by the Chairman of the Penal Law Commission, Richard Bartlett.

6. Ibid., p. 69.

7. The Challenge of Crime in a Free Society. A Report by the President's Commission on Law Enforcement and the Administration of Justice. U.S. Government Printing Office. (Washington, D.C.: February 1967) p. 142.

8. Governor Nelson A. Rockefeller's Conference on Crime. Proceedings, April 1966. Statement by Richard Bartlett, p. 69.

9. The Official Report of the New York State Special Commission on Attica (The McKay Commission Report) (New York: A Bantam Book, 1972), pp. 94-97.

10. Chapter 1080 of the Laws of 1968 allowed the "leasing of state institutions to cities or counties for the confinement of prisoners. . . so that in the case of a civil disorder, any sentenced persons. . . could be transferred to state correctional institutions if local detention facilities were strained to capacity." In, Office of Legislative Research Facts 1968, Crime, Corrections and Criminal Justice, p. 16.

11. Tom Wicker, A Time to Die (New York: Quadrangle/The New York Times Book Co., 1975), p. 148.

12. Governor Nelson A. Rockefeller's Conference on Crime. Proceedings, December 15, 1967. Statement by Attorney General Louis Lefkowitz, p. 4.

13. Wicker, A Time to Die, p. 149.

14. Ibid.

15. Robert Connery, "Nelson A. Rockefeller as Governor" in Governing New York State: The Rockefeller Years, Edited by Robert Connery and Gerald Benjamin (New York: The Academy of Political Science, May 1974) pp. 6-7.

16. Ibid., p. 35.

17. Governor's Crime Control Program. Report of the Office of Legislative Research, April 9, 1968, p. 2 (Mimeograph)

18. Ibid.

19. Message of Governor Nelson A. Rockefeller to the Legislature, January 6, 1965, p. 48.

20. Ibid.

21. Governor Nelson A. Rockefeller's Conference on Crime. Proceedings, April 21-22, 1966. "Panel on Citizen Involvement in the Administration of Justice", pp. 103-25.

22. Governor Nelson A. Rockefeller's Conference on Crime. Proceedings, December 15, 1967, Table of Contents, pp. iv-vi.

23. Conference on Crime. Proceedings, December 15, 1967, pp. 4-5.

24. Ibid., p. 3.

25. Message of Governor Nelson A. Rockefeller to the Legislature, January 3, 1968, p. 8.

26. Office of Legislative Research Facts 1966. Crime, Corrections, and Criminal Justice, p. 2. (Mimeograph)

27. Office of Legislative Research Facts 1968. Crime, Corrections, and Criminal Justice, p. 34.

28. Alan Chartock, "Narcotic Addiction: The Politics of Frustration" in Governing New York State: The Rockefeller Years, ed. Benjamin and Connery, p. 242.

29. Ibid.

30. Ibid., p. 243.

31. Office of Legislative Research Facts 1968. Crime, Corrections and Criminal Justice, p. 39.

32. Ibid., p. 35.

33. Ibid., p. 38.

34. Ibid., p. 39.

35. Richard A. McGee, Prisons and Politics (Lexington, Mass.: D.C. Heath and Co., 1981) p. 125.

36. New York State Correction - Executive Budget, 1972-1973, p. 451.

37. Chartock, "Narcotic Addiction: The Politics of Frustration", p. 244

38. Office of Legislative Research Facts 1968. Crime, Corrections and Criminal Justice, pp. 36-37.

39. For a discussion of treatment of deviants according to class, see Harry Elmer Barnes, The Story of Punishment Second Edition, Revised (Montclair, N.J.: Patterson Smith, 1972, originally published in 1930) Chapter 4, "Transportation as a Method of Punishment", pp. 68-92. See also, Hollingshead and Redlich, Social Class and Mental Illness (New York: John Wiley and Sons, 1958) and David Greenberg, Editor, Crime and Capitalism (Palo Alto: Mayfield Publishing Company, 1981)

40. New York State Correction - Executive Budget. State Purposes Budget, 1969-1970, p. 274.

41. Statement by Senator Jacob Javits in the Troy Record, 2 November 1970: "Senator Jacob Javits said. . . narcotic addicts should be treated as medical cases rather than as criminals."

42. New York State Correction - Executive Budget, State Purposes Budget 1969-1970, p. 275.

43. Ibid., pp. 274-75

44. Confidential source in correctional administration.

45. New York State Correction - Executive Budget, 1966-1967.

46. Interviews with Donald Goff, former Secretary of the Correctional Association of New York, October 1972 - April 1973.

47. Preliminary Report of the Governor's Special Committee on Criminal Offenders, June 1968, p. 12.

48. Office of Legislative Research Facts 1968. Crime,

Corrections and *Criminal* Justice, p. 25.

49.   Interviews   with   Frances   Kernohan,   Community   Service
Society, March 3, 1975; Austin MacCormick, Osborne Association,
May 2,   1974;   Don   McEvoy   and   Gladys   Burleigh,   National
Conference of Christians and Jews, March 1975.

50.   Preliminary Report of the Governor's Special Committee on
Criminal Offenders, June 1968, p. 14.

51.   New   York   State   Legislative   Annual,   p.   358   Baxstrom   v.
Herold 383 US 107 (1966); Specht v. Patterson 87 S. Ct. 1209
(1967) U.S. v. Maroney 355 F 2d 302 (3rd cir 1966)

52.   Robert Connery and Gerald Benjamin, Rockefeller of New
York, (Ithaca: Cornell University Press., 1979), p. 12.

53.   Preliminary Report of the Governor's Special Committee on
Criminal Offenders, June 1968, pp. 12-13.

54.   Interview with Vito Ternullo, former head of the Division of
Education in the Department of Correction, May 9, 1974.

55.   Connery, "Nelson A. Rockefeller as Governor", p. 8.

56.   Ibid.

57.   Interview with John Delaney, Assistant Director of the
Governor's Special Committee on Criminal Offenders, December 1,
1974.

58.   A Report of the Senate Committee on Penal Institutions for
the 1967 Legislative Session, March 30, 1967, p. 3 (Mimeograph)

59.   1967 Youth and Correction Legislation in New York State.
Report of the Committee on Youth and Correction of the
Community Service Society, September 1967, p. viii.

60.   Ibid., p. 33.

61.   Preliminary Report of the Governor's Special Committee on
Criminal Offenders, June 1968, p. 61.

62.   Minutes of the Proceedings of a Budget Hearing on the
Department of Correction held by the Senate Committee on Finance
and the Assembly Ways and Means Committee in the Assembly
Parlor, Capitol Building, Albany, New York, February 16, 1970,
p. 10. (Mimeograph)

63.   The Official Report of the New York State Special Commission

on Attica, pp. 116-122

64. WCBS Television Broadcast, August 31, 1969, 11:30 A.M. Interview with George McGrath, New York City Commissioner of Correction and John R. Dunne, State Senator. Discussion topic was titled, "New York City's Overcrowded Jails". Transcript, pp. 9-10.

65. Minutes of the Proceedings of a Budget Hearing on Correctional Services, held by the Senate Finance Committee and the Assembly Ways and Means Committee in the Assembly Parlor, The Capitol, Albany, New York, February 10, 1971, p. 56. (Mimeograph)

66. Public Hearing in New York City by the Governor's Special Committee on Criminal Offenders. No page notation. (Mimeograph)

67. Interview with Frances Kernohan, Community Service Society, Staff Associate. Committee on Youth and Correction, March 3, 1975.

68. Interview with John Delaney, Assistant Director of the Governor's Special Committee on Criminal Offenders, December 1, 1974.

69. Interview with Vito Ternullo, May 9, 1974.

70. Interview with Matthew Fitzgerald, former Director of the New York State Council of the National Council on Crime and Delinquency, March 20, 1975.

71. Ibid.

72. Ibid.

73. Ibid.

74. The Official Report of the New York State Special Commission on Attica, p. 131.

75. Preliminary Report of the Governor's Special Committee on Criminal Offenders, June 1968, p. 13.

76. Interviews with Donald Goff, October 1972 - April 1973.

77. Interviews with John R. Dunne while serving as staff assistant, September 1967 - May 1969.

78. Ibid.

79.   1967 Youth and Correction Legislation in New York State
September 1967. Community Service Society, p. viii.

80.   A Report of the Senate Committee on Penal Institutions for
the 1967 Legislative Session, March 30, 1967, p. 4.

81.   Connery, "Nelson A. Rockefeller as Governor", p. 10.

82.   Transcript of the Hearings of the New York State Senate
Committee on Penal Institutions re: Work Release Legislation,
March 28, 1968, Albany, New York, pp. 39-70. (Mimeograph)

83.   Ibid., pp. 2-3

84.   Barbara A. Lavin while Staff Assistant to John R. Dunne,
September 1967 - May 1969.

85.   Ibid.

86.   Statement by Russell G. Oswald in Minutes of the Correction
Department Budget Hearing, February 29, 1972, in the Assembly
Parlor before the Senate Finance Committee and the Assembly
Ways and Means Committee, Albany, New York, pp. 26-27.
(Mimeograph)

87.   Barbara A. Lavin while staff assistant to John R. Dunne,
September 1967 - May 1969.

88.   Interview with Russell G. Oswald, former Commissioner of
the Department of Correctional Services, March 19, 1975.

89.   For a discussion of Legislative involvement in Corrections,
see Richard A. McGee Prisons and Politics (Lexington, Mass.:
D.C. Heath and Co., 1981) Chapter 3, pp. 27-40. and Erik Olin
Wright The Politics of Punishment (New York: Harper and Row.,
1973) Chapter 13 pp. 262-280.

90.   Minutes of the Correction Department Budget Hearing,
February 16, 1970, p. 47.

91.   1967 Youth and Correction Legislation in New York State
September 1967. Community Service Society, pp. iv-v.

92.   Minutes of the Correction Department Budget Hearing,
February 29, 1968, in the Assembly Parlor before the Senate
Finance Committee and the Assembly Ways and Means Committee,
Albany, New York, pp. 57-58. (Mimeograph)

93.   Ibid., p. 67.

94. Interview with Russell G. Oswald, March 19, 1975.

95. Ibid.

96. Ibid.

CHAPTER IV

THE PROMISE OF REFORM

Introduction

Chapter three described how the correctional arena, formerly a monolithic system controlled by the bureaucracy under the leadership of McGinnis, was in the late 1960s being forced to accommodate the intrusion of various Gubernatorial study commissions. As indicated in Chapter three, the study commissions, although in name composed of top level bureaucrats, actually enjoyed a certain amount of independence since the commissions' staff had been appointed directly by the Governor and were therefore ultimately responsible to him. (1) Thus, the final reports of the study commissions were at times antithetical to bureaucratic interests. (2) This was especially true of correctional interests.

Therefore, the decision - making power of the bureaucracy was especially threatened in 1970 when recommendations stemming from the Governor's Special Committee on Criminal Offenders were passed into law and resulted in the amalgamation of the Departments of Correction and Parole into a new Department of Correctional Services, under the Chairmanship of the former head of Parole, Russell G. Oswald.

In the early 1970s this erosion of bureaucratic power was further hastened by the intrusion of new actors and interests. Among these new interests was a socially and politically aware inmate group whose membership transcended the traditional radical, religious or ethnic boundaries of previous groups. Within this grouping of "new inmates" were Blacks, Whites and Spanish-speaking, the products of various social forces prevalent in the 1960s. For the Blacks, the civil rights movement of the early 1960s, the "black power" protest movement of the late 1960s, and the eventual formation of political/religious groupings, such as the Black Muslims or the Black Panthers, had created a lasting awareness of political realities. For Whites, the student protests and the Vietnam anti-war protests of the 1960s had resulted in a "new wave of protests and backlash. . . ending in blood in Chicago and Kent State."(3) And the Spanish-speaking, politicized by the 1960s, also demanded recognition of their Spanish culture and an end to discrimination against them. (4)

Thus many inmates, but not all, came to accept the rhetoric of the New Left and identified themselves as "political prisoners", meaning "they claimed that responsibility for their actions belonged not to them but to a society which had failed to provide adequate housing, equal educational opportunities and an equal opportunity to compete in American life."(5)   Although these inmates in general identified as victims of society, they were not committed to a radical political ideology of revolution as were another small group of predominantly white, self-styled anti-establishment revolutionaries, incarcerated for the bombing of public buildings.(6)   This new breed of inmate came to prison with a shared heritage of violent political protest and was totally unlike the traditional inmate the correctional bureaucracy was accustomed to dealing with.

> In contrast to this new breed of inmate were the older inmates - black, white and Spanish-speaking who had come to accept prison conditions: they made few demands upon the officials, proclaimed at most their own innocence but not society's guilt, kept their frustration and anger to themselves and accepted the word of the guards as law. Many. . . expressed deep antagonism toward younger inmates who were not prepared to "do their own time" and insisted on defying authority.(7)

Thus the prisons in New York State in the 1970s contained both groups of inmates.   But the new breed of radical inmate, from urban areas and highly politicized before incarceration in state penal facilities, was numerous and active.   From 1966 to 1970, 73 percent of all inmates received in New York State Prisons came from the urban areas of the state; 43 percent were under the age of thirty; 33 percent were admitted drug users; and 65 percent were Black and Puerto Rican.(8)

It was almost inevitable that this politicized inmate of the 1970s would seek the court system for redress of his grievances; for the courts had already been the successful focal point of civil rights cases a decade earlier.   Thus the courts became a battleground between inmate and custodial interests in the 1970s.

The barrage of prisoner rights cases which flooded the courts in the early 1970s were either writs compiled by "inmate-lawyers" on their own initiative, or by some of the recent law school graduates, products of a civil rights era who "were ready to champion the rights of prisoners, viewed as inextricably linked with the rights of students, draftees, and the mentally ill - all seen as subject to the arbitrary rule of administrative despotism."(9)   Thus lawyers from Legal Aid Societies, New York Civil Liberties Union and the American Civil Liberties Union assisted the inmates in the presentation of prisoner rights suits in Federal Court. A complete analysis of the involvement of these legal groups is not within the purview of this study. Therefore, our attention will remain focused on the activities of those groups already identified as the central protagonists through time in the correctional arena, namely, the religious/social reformers, correctional bureaucracy, business and economic interests and inmate groups.

The focus of this chapter will be the young, politicized inmates, already identified as the "new breed" incarcerated within New York State prisons, and government response to their demands. Data will be organized and analyzed according to the following schema: 1) federal court involvement in the New York State prison system; 2) riots within the New York City prison system; 3) disturbances at the state prisons of Auburn and Attica and 4) involvement of investigative study commissions, such as the McKay Commission. An analysis of the involvement of the four primary interest groups will be interwoven throughout.

New Actors Enter the Correctional Arena

Federal Court Involvement in the New York State Prison System

As has been shown, prior to the mid-1960s the penal system in New York State was an enclosed system, the domain of the correctional bureaucracy and not subject to review by any outside power source. However in the 1970s, the Courts became involved in state penal conditions, a reversal of an historical, judicial position of non-interference in state penal matters.

Traditionally, the federal courts had determined that state prison conditions were not within their jurisdiction and consequently determined a "hands off" policy concerning state penal matters. The Federal Court (2nd District) had ruled as late as 1969 in Bethea v. Crouse that

> we have consistently adhered to the so-called "hands-off" doctrine in matters of prison administration according to which we have said that the basic responsibility for the control and management of penal institutions including the discipline, treatment and care of those confined, lies with the responsible administrative agency and is not subject to judicial review unless exercised in such a manner as to constitute clear abuse or caprice on the

part of prison officials. (10)

And according to former Commissioner of Correctional Services, Russell G. Oswald, when decisions were handled by state courts, the usually conservative state courts ruled in favor of the correctional administration. (11)

However, the late 1960s witnessed an emerging social awareness among minority groups, racial unrest in the cities, and the emergence of persons interested in penal social justice from a legal/political rather than from a religious standpoint. According to Russell G. Oswald, with the passage of the Federal Civil Rights Act of 1968, cases formerly heard by the state courts were now being heard in federal courts and the federal courts, more liberal by nature, were beginning to rule in favor of the inmate. (12)

According to many observers, the first significant case concerning the rights of inmates was Judge Julius Hoffman's decision in the <u>Inmates</u> of <u>Cook County Jail</u> <u>v</u>. <u>Tierney</u> (1968). In this instance, Judge Hoffman upheld a Civil Rights claim by jail inmates who alleged in a class action suit that they were subjected to: inadequate food, light, heat, sanitation and medical care; lack of recreational facilities; lack of facilities for conferences with attorneys; lack of privacy; overcrowding and exposure to beatings, sexual attacks and other dangers resulting from an inadequate guard system. (13) The case was settled on assurances by the defendant officials that they were effecting fundamental changes. Although the inmates achieved no specific tangible benefits, they had achieved one major victory, the right of access to the courts.

Additional court cases in 1969 and 1970 further secured this right of access. Thus, prison officials could not confiscate or delay legal pleadings or correspondence addressed to the courts, nor could they punish inmates for bringing suit against the prison administration. (14) And in 1969, the Supreme Court held in <u>Johnson</u> <u>v</u>. <u>Avery</u> that unless prison officials provide reasonable legal assistance to inmates, they may not validly enforce a regulation barring inmates from helping one another with legal work. (15)

In New York State, the federal court decisions involving a Black Muslim, "jailhouse lawyer" inmate named Martin Sostre clearly indicated the extent of federal court involvement in the administration of state prisons in the early 1970s. These court decisions not only set the stage for the further political and legal involvement of inmates in the correctional arena but were subsequently viewed by custodial interests as an encroachment on bureaucratic control of the prison system.

Although other federal court decisions asserted judicial involvement in the administration of the New York State prison system,(16) none received the publicity of the Sostre decisions and likewise none were to have as visible a political effect on the incarcerated minorities in New York State Prisons.

Sostre had been imprisoned originally in the 1960s and while in prison had initiated federal civil rights litigation which had resulted in an expanded recognition and protection of religious freedom for Black Muslims in jail, including the right to gather for corporate religious services and to consult a minister of their faith.(17) Meanwhile, other federal cases in other districts had established the right to subscribe to religious literature, including Muhammed Speaks to wear unobtrusive religious medals and other symbols; to have prepared a special diet required by the Muslim religion; and to correspond with any spiritual leader.(18) These were privileges that for the most part had long been accorded the traditional Protestant and Catholic prison inmates. But because of the close unity of the Muslims and their religious ideology which was viewed by prison administrators as hostile and inflammatory (anti-white), most prison administrators had banned the practice of Islam or imposed tight restrictions on the Muslims.(19)

Sostre had been returned to prison in 1968 on a drug charge and was subsequently held in Greenhaven prison in solitary confinement. Although no written notice was given to Sostre of the charges against him, nor was an administrative hearing held to determine his guilt or innocence,(20) Sostre was kept in solitary confinement for over one year on a restricted diet, permitted to shower and shave with hot water only once weekly, denied permission to work, refused access to the prison library and not allowed to read newspapers, watch movies, or participate in educational or vocational training programs.(21) Sostre filed suit in federal court, alleging that such confinement was unconstitutional and that therefore he was entitled to both damages and injunctive relief under the Civil Rights Act of 1871.

On July 2, 1969, Federal Judge Constance Baker Motley issued a temporary restraining order requiring prison officials to release Sostre from solitary confinement. After a full evidentiary hearing, Judge Motley found that the treatment of Martin Sostre was unconstitutional(22) and awarded Sostre compensatory damages of $25.00 for each day that Sostre had been held in segregation (372 days), a total of $9,300 and an additional $3,270 for punitive damages.(23) The Sostre decision was subsequently reviewed by the U.S. Court of Appeals, 2nd Circuit, which upheld Motley's determination that Sostre's treatment was unconstitutional(24) and while upholding the payment of compensatory damages ($9,300), the Court of Appeals reversed the $3,270 award of punitive damages, indicating that the deterrent impact of a punitive award would be minimal. (25) This was the first time that monetary damages of either a compensatory or punitive nature had been awarded to an inmate of a state penal institution for improper disciplinary treatment by the correctional bureaucracy. (26)

As might be expected, the New York State correctional bureaucracy and administration viewed these federal court decisions as extraordinarily threatening to their control of the institutions. (27) The correctional administrators perceived that their control was being eroded by the courts. (28) As has been noted,

> the reaction of prison guards to the Sostre decision was immediate and intense. Like the police officers who condemned decisions of the Supreme Court on criminal due process, they took up the cry of "handcuffing the police" and "coddling the criminals". Guards almost universally felt that the courts were interfering in matters in which they had no competence. . . . The decision was wrong, guards felt, and they not the judges - would have to live with the consequences. (29)

Russell G. Oswald had stated that

> interjection of the courts ultimately can lead to conditions whereby the courts will assume all control over correctional programs. Should this occur, the result would be to take the professionals out of the profession. If the courts substitute their judgment for that of parole boards, they will get what they deserve. (30)

Thus, the correctional administration and bureaucracy found themselves in direct conflict with inmate interests as defined and protected by the federal courts. But the inmates did not rely solely on the federal court system to achieve change in the penal system. The 1970s witnessed increasing violence on the part of the inmate.

Riots within the New York City Prison System

Violence first erupted in the New York City prison system

80

during the summer of 1970. In August, more than one thousand inmates took control of sections of the Manhattan House of Detention for Men (Tombs) and held eight correction officers as hostages.(31) Later in October of 1970, riots again broke out in all five of the city's detention facilities. The inmate demands in both cases were the same: speedy trials, lower bail(32) and better living conditions.(33) Overcrowded conditions at the Tombs at the time of the riot necessitated the housing of two or three men in a cell constructed for one.(34) In general, the New York City correctional administration and many of the correctional officers conceded that the inmate grievances were legitimate.(35) Acting Warden Arthur Singerman had stated, that "all of the inmate grievances are real, except the charge of systemized brutality (by correctional officers)." (36)

Inmates claimed that the only reason for the Tombs riot was to "reach the public" and any survey of the newspapers at this time (August 1970) indicated that in this they were successful. One of the slogans shouted by inmates was "We want justice now. . . . We want The News." (37) The inmates of the 1970s viewed the media as crucial in publicizing their demands, in gaining the support of that mass public predisposed to minority rights, and in mobilizing the Blacks and Puerto Ricans in the larger society outside the prisons. In the Tombs riot, the inmates demanded television coverage of their negotiations with city officials.(38) At Attica likewise, inmates demanded the presence of newsmen of their own choice during the negotiations between inmates and officials.(39) The hope was that support could be mobilized in the larger society outside prison walls and that concessions to inmate demands made by prison officials, in public, during the riot, could not as easily be rescinded after the prison had been returned to normalcy. Such publicity did attract the attention of State Senator John R. Dunne, who was characterized in the press as a "Crusader for Prison Reforms".(40)

Although not aligned with the religious/social reformers on all issues, Dunne shared many of their concerns for humane, just treatment of inmates.(41) But it must also be noted that Dunne was committed to working within the legislative/executive system and was therefore sympathetic to the problems confronting correctional officials and administrators due to a lack of public funds to insure a humane, just treatment of inmates.(42) Therefore, Dunne cannot easily be characterized as representing either reform or correctional interests. On the issue of the Tombs riot however, John R. Dunne may be viewed as supportive of reform interests, although the reformers were never wholeheartedly to support Dunne.(43)

At a series of public hearings held after the riots at the

Tombs, Dunne subpoenaed inmates and reluctant public officials including the New York City Commissioner of Corrections, George McGrath. Although the correctional administration had agreed that the inmate demands were legitimate, both Mayor Lindsay and George McGrath were violently opposed to Dunne's public hearings on the matter. Penal matters had always been handled internally and not in a public forum; thus, Dunne was accused of staging a "shabby personal publicity circus; of keeping the pot at a boil, giving militants outside the institution and their cohorts both the climate and the platform they need to pursue their course of agitation."(44)

Thus penal issues became public issues much to the dismay of both city and state correctional administrators. As a result of federal court decisions and publicity given to inmate concerns, power in the correctional arena appeared to be suddenly shifting away from the correctional bureaucracy toward the inmate groups within the prisons. As Commissioner Paul McGinnis had stated,

> the federal courts have taken away many of the tools administrators used to help keep control over the inmates and institutions. That combined with an influx of a new breed of inmate has produced an ugly situation and threatens the penal system. If it keeps up like this, then blood is going to run at many of the institutions.(45)

McGinnis continued,

> inmates today are younger, organized, more militant, more violent and more demanding. They don't consider themselves thieves, rapists or murderers. Today they feel they are political prisoners jailed by a repressive society. . . . Black Panthers and Young Lords (a militant Puerto Rican group) are the most vocal and violent of the militant groups inside prison walls. . . . There have been indicators that. . . disturbances are planned for other institutions within the system. There is reason to believe that inmates receive instructions from outside.(46)

But whether this seeming shift of power was permanent or temporary, real or chimerical, will be analyzed throughout this chapter. Certainly as McGinnis had stated, the prisoner of the

1960s and 1970s was very different from the inmate of the 1920s who had organized within the prison to effect such changes within the system as better food, more sanitary living conditions and increased recreational activities.(47) The prisoners of the 1960s and 1970s, as can be demonstrated in the Tombs riot, protested not only against conditions within the prison institutions but against social conditions outside the prison as well as against a judicial system which they felt discriminated against the poor. Thus, attempts were made to link the plight of the prisoners to that of the racial poor within the broader society.

As Wendell Wade, one of the founders of the Black Panther Party had stated,

> the prisons are now filling with political prisoners, those brothers who were active in opposing the occupation of the black community by the fascist police force and its domination by the exploitative businessmen and tyrannical politicians. . . . (48)

This analysis of the political situation by the militant groups such as the Black Panthers, Young Lords and Black Muslims in particular, outside the prisons, as well as by the inmates was also noted in a New York Times article of October 8, 1970. The article noted that the abundance of slogans and revolutionary rhetoric suggested a growing political consciousness among inmates.(49) In the same article, John R. Dunne likewise suggested that,

> such groups as the Panthers, and the Young Lords might have been largely instrumental in channeling the discontent into demonstrations. . . . Their rhetoric in general terms about social inequalities has found a receptive audience among the inmates, almost all of whom feel they have been mistreated.(50)

And a member of the Central Committee of the Young Lords Party continued this theme, "the Puerto Rican brothers inside identify with us just like the black brothers identify with the Panthers."(51) According to this activist, increasingly, the inmates saw their situation in terms of systematic social oppression.(52)

Deputy Commissioner of the New York City Department of Correction, Al Castro, crystallized the problems thus created for the correctional staff,

One thing is certain, persons who run penal institutions of the future will have to be near experts in politics, psychology, sociology, and even revolutionary confrontation tactics. . . . This is a different breed of inmate. . . . Professional radicals and revolutionaries are forming the nucleus of leadership in prisons around the nation. . . . They are willing to riot. . . . Try to discipline them and they say, "You're violating my civil rights."(53)

This was a new breed of inmate, better organized than in the past and educated in the "New Left" radical ideology that identified them as "political prisoners" in a materialistic, capitalist society. According to one observer,

one source of leadership was the middle class, often college educated, inmate convicted on drug charges or draft evasion. . . a second and more important source was the Black Panthers and Black Muslims. . . often in prison because their political activism had led to confrontations with the police. Already motivated by their political ideology and experienced in organizing political protests on the outside, they find prisons to be well suited for their organizing skills and political aims.(54)

Thus the prison riot in New York City should be viewed in political terms as were the urban riots of the 1960s; that is, as an attempt to bring to the attention of the public-at-large conditions which were viewed as intolerable by groups largely outside the mainstream of being able to institute political change effectively by the traditional means of lobbying techniques, election of sympathetic political candidates and advertising campaigns. Increasingly therefore, as Michael Lipsky has noted, "the powerless have resorted to protest and often violent protest as a means of publicizing and bargaining for social change."(55) How successful they were will be demonstrated by an analysis of governmental response both to inmate demands and to the demands of the correctional bureaucracy who believed that detailed preparations for the Tombs uprising had been made by a hard core of political activists.(56)

In the aftermath of the Tombs riot, the correctional officers demanded and obtained, payment of back overtime which had not been dispensed in six months, a more extensive in-service training program and orientation for new officers (increased from one week to six weeks), and new riot protection equipment.(57) The President of the New York City correctional officers union (the Correctional Officers Benevolent Association) requested an increased staff of 700 correction officers; he obtained 300.(58) Also in response to correction officer demands, a new riot policy declared that other correction officers would immediately be called into the prisons to quell disturbances and to retake hostages or areas occupied by rebellious inmates.(59) Thus, the correctional officers emerged from the riot in a stronger custodial position than that present before the riot; tangible benefits by way of increased security measures and additional personnel were thus accorded custodial interests.

However, nothing appeared in either legislative enactments or internal prison policy which would demonstrate an amelioration of the prisoners' condition at this time, despite expressions of concern from politicians stating that the problems would be looked into.

Additional funds were requested by the correctional administration and bureaucracy as well as by the Mayor for a new light security Jail which would ease overcrowding and thus provide better security. However, the new jail proposal was vehemently opposed by the National Conference of Black Lawyers, Planners for Equal Opportunity and other groups who classified all of the city prisons including the proposed new jail as "concentration camps for the city's poor."(60) Plans for the new jail were dismissed and as an alternative solution to the city's overcrowding, more and more city prisoners were transferred to state penal institutions. One of the prisoners so transferred was later to play a prominent role in the Attica Prison Riot.(61) Paul McGinnis, Commissioner of the New York State Department of Correction, was very much opposed to this transfer of over six hundred sentenced, rebellious city inmates to state prison facilities; but, McGinnis was overruled by the Governor.(62) Thus, a more militant prisoner was admitted to the state system with ramifications as yet unforeseen in August of 1970.

Prison Riot in the New York State Penal System: Auburn

Demonstrations soon spread to the state prison system. In November of 1970, the correctional administration of Auburn State Prison was likewise confronted with rebelling inmates. On November 4, 1970, four hundred inmates took possession of a major portion of the prison for nine hours and held more than thirty-five guards as hostages. Six correction officers were

85

injured and required hospital treatment. However, as in the New York City riots, the threat of force was enough to drive inmates back to their cells and obtain the release of the hostages.(63)

Again as in the New York City situation, demands by the inmates for better living conditions and for an end to harassment and brutality by the guards were met with counter demands by the correctional officers for increased security measures, additional correctional officers, improved training programs for the officers as well as creation of a separate facility for "hard core" prisoners.(64)

McGinnis had responded to the rioting inmates at Auburn by placing the total population in their cells for a period of weeks. Seventy-two were still in confinement when Russell G. Oswald assumed office in January of 1971. Federal suits had been initiated on behalf of the seventy-two inmates by lawyers for the NAACP Legal Defense Fund and the New York Civil Liberties Union, who contended that due process guarantees had been violated.(65) Six inmates had already been indicted for their role in the November Auburn riot. Other inmates had written to lawyers and activist groups telling of beatings and gassing by the guards.(66)

The state of these Auburn inmates was given considerable press coverage and they were being referred to in the press and among civil libertarians as "The Auburn Six" or "The Auburn Seventy-Two".(67) The cause of the Auburn inmates was taken up by such militant groups as Youth Against Fascism and the War, a militant anti-war remnant of the Vietnam opposition. Busloads of protesters came to Auburn to demonstrate outside the prison walls for the release of the Auburn Six, the Auburn Seventy-Two and all "political prisoners".(68)

Correctional authorities on the other hand, stated that these inmates were revolutionaries committed to the destruction of the entire prison system.(69) In the tense atmosphere created by the attempted riot inside the prison and in view of the continuing "propaganda" both inside and outside the prison walls for what the correctional administration considered militant revolutionary action, the prison officials declared a state of emergency. Under it, officials reduced the length of recreation periods and kept men in segregation for indefinite periods. For the first three months after the riot, nearly all 1,600 inmates were confined to their cells and were given only two meals a day.(70) In six months, Auburn had three different Wardens.

When Russell G. Oswald assumed leadership of the new Department of Correctional Services in January of 1971, he inherited, according to one former department official, "a department that had stood still for thirteen years. . . regarding the knowledge of and training of inmates and the knowledge of and training of guards."(71) The former official continued, "there had been no full staff meeting of Division heads for the last ten years of McGinnis' administration. . . . McGinnis did nothing, kept meetings down and never held or initiated meetings."(72) Oswald, according to many correctional officials, reaped the problems stemming from McGinnis' inaction.(73)

In transitional briefings, Oswald had received a report on penal conditions from McGinnis. Oswald has stated that,

> McGinnis became quite emotional and pointed out that because of lack of attention money-wise to the correctional program, institution after institution was a powder keg. . . . McGinnis also said that he had made a request for additional money, but that it was not provided. This was the time of the Taxpayers Revolt in New York State.(74)

Thus both the Governor and the Legislative leaders failed to provide the public funds deemed necessary by McGinnis.

Russell G. Oswald understood well the problems he would face as commissioner and is reported to have twice turned down the Governor's request that he head the newly created Department of Correctional Services.(75) Aside from the situation already mentioned within the prisons, there would be administrative difficulties in coordinating the work of the two formerly autonomous bureaucracies of Corrections and Parole. An uneasy truce had previously existed between Corrections and Parole with each blaming the other for the failures returned to prison with new convictions or with parole violations. Now, despite the fact that neither bureaucracy was to lose job positions, the merging of responsibility for institutional and field supervision of convicted offenders in one agency with unified direction and leadership from the former Chairman of Parole would no doubt lead to some anxiety especially within the correctional bureaucracy. The correctional staff considered Oswald as a reformer, who was willing to compromise their concern for security and custody in order to implement rehabilitative programs.(76)

On the other hand, the religious/social reformers did not wholeheartedly support Oswald either. Frances Kernohan, staff associate for Community Service Society, chagrined that the reformers had not been consulted by the Governor on Oswald's appointment, stated "we would not have supported Oswald

87

anyway, despite his social work background, because he was as archaic as McGinnis. . . . "(77)

Thus Oswald began his new appointment as he has stated, "with some misgivings." (78) He did not have a firm base of support either inside or outside the Department.

The continuing decrease in state prison population resulted in the state retention of some 2,200 commitments to the Narcotic Addiction Control Commission and some 3,200 City of New York cases.(79) According to Oswald, these past agreements to accept NACC and New York City inmates "have painted us in a very tight corner that make short range needed physical changes almost impossible."(80) Oswald continued,

> concurrent with this, is the outbreak of hard core militancy involving a relatively small percentage of the inmate population. . . under normal conditions, these militants would be transferred to other facilities. . . but through varying and wide range court decisions, any transfer of ringleaders forces us to place them not in segregation but in the general population where they continue to create intensive problems.(81)

Oswald also noted that the Wardens of the prison institutions felt they were rapidly losing control. They felt beset by a small hard core group of radicals and militants and liberal attorneys pressing issues against them.(82)

Oswald has stated that while he was committed essentially to a rehabilitative approach utilizing psychological treatment and social work in medium security facilities - an approach totally different from McGinnis who had emphasized secure custody of inmates, the traditional approach approved by the New York State electorate - that even he, in an effort to accommodate the anxiety on the part of the Superintendents (Wardens) and correction officers, as well as to subdue the militancy of some inmates, had studied the advisability of developing a "maxi-maximum institution within an institution that would nullify the militant leadership and its philosophy of revolution and, at the same time, permit us to institute an intensive program for redirection for this group to change or modify attitudes and actions."(83) Thus Oswald sought a compromise between the historical commitment to custody accepted by correctional officers and Superintendents as the means of dealing with troublesome inmates, and the rehabilitative approach to which he himself was committed.

Oswald also felt that his and the department's capability were being diminished by the legal groups, who were seeking prisoner civil rights and abstract perfect justice, as can be demonstrated in his comments before the 1971 Legislative Budget Hearing.

> With this constant barrage of ACLU lawyers and their thrust to enforce civil rights action, it seems to me very definitely that we are going to need some lawyers in our own system. . . . At the present time, we have only two lawyers in the department and. . . every day there are at least eight or ten more law suits instituted against us and to which we must address ourselves. . . . Frankly, we are like a minor league team playing against a professional team. Our legal talent against the talent of all of these ACLU lawyers, and law school professors and various law students and so on, it is all stacked against the administration and we don't have adequate legal help.(84)

Meanwhile propaganda was continuing inside and outside the prisons among the more militant radical groups. And despite all of these conflicting demands for policy changes, funds were not forthcoming for change, as can be demonstrated in the following analysis of the Greenberg Report.

In April of 1971, a study of the Correction Department budget was begun by the staff of the Minority Senate Finance Committee. According to staff associate, Don Clifford,

> fiscally, the Corrections budget presented no problem, it was the cheapest budget around, but the investment was being poured down the drain. There seemed to be no concern with the inmate as he was coming out of the "rehabilitative" programs and returning to society.(85)

Therefore, a study of the Correction Department budget was begun; but, according to Clifford, very little information or assistance could be obtained from the Department itself. Nevertheless what finally emerged in August of 1971 was a very thorough document detailing the custody-oriented penal system that in many ways was more harsh and punitive than when the system originated in the mid 1800s.(86)

Again according to Clifford, it became evident that

> the custodial staff controlled the
> Department and although there was no
> formal union prior to 1968, there was an
> informal union insofar as son replaced
> father who had replaced grandfather as
> guard at the institutions. The
> Superintendent or Warden of the prison
> moved up through the ranks and the
> entire town of Elmira, Attica or Auburn
> controlled the prison through personnel
> allotments. (87)

The Greenberg Report, as it was known from the Chairman of the
Senate Finance Minority, Senator Samuel Greenberg, detailed the
impact of custodial over rehabilitative considerations.

In summary, the seventy-nine page report noted that

> the state correctional institutions have for
> too long been controlled by an antiquated
> policy of isolation and confinement to the
> virtual neglect of rehabilitation. There
> are absolutely no full time psychiatrists
> or psychologists authorized for state
> prisons. . . . Professional education and
> counseling staff comprise less than 10% of
> the total authorized staffing of these
> correctional institutions but correctional
> guards command almost 70%. The
> irrelevancy of this policy is symbolized by
> correctional facilities whose sites were
> chosen in a by-gone era and now serve
> only to reinforce punishment and deter
> rehabilitation. (88)

Greenberg had praise for Oswald's efforts but noted that,

> the words of one Commissioner are not
> enough if they are not backed up by the
> support of the Administration he serves.
> The Commissioner has been forced to seek
> federal aid for rehabilitation programs
> similar to those which the Governor
> allowed to be cut from the 1971-72
> Executive Budget. The Republican
> controlled Legislature cut $256,000 out of
> the Executive Budget for a residential
> treatment program. The commissioner has

now requested the Federal
Government. . . to sponsor a regional
correctional facility. . . which has similar
program inputs. And the cutbacks for
1971-1972 are not an isolated example of
the Administration's neglect of its
correctional program. In the preceding
twelve fiscal years under Governor
Rockefeller, appropriation levels for
program improvements in correctional
institutions have increased less than three
percent annually and if salary increments
for personnel service are deducted, these
increases would probably be less than one
percent.(89)

In conclusion, the Senator called for a meaningful rehabilitation
program in the institutions.(90)

Ironically the report was released only several weeks prior
to the Attica riot. Clifford, Greenberg's staff associate, has
denied that there was any personal political motivation behind the
report and in fact, Senator Greenberg was nearing retirement age
and contemplated a Florida retirement. According to Clifford,
Greenberg hoped for a favorable response from the legislature.
For although essentially a reform piece, the Greenberg report was
also intended as an "inside" legislative document. Clifford has
stated that "no reform groups rallied to the support of the
Greenberg Report, but then we did not seek the support from
outside groups."(91) Nevertheless, the report was so widely
circulated within the legislature among staff and legislators, it
seems inconceivable that the reformers were not aware of the
report. And the action oriented press which was interested in
the sensationalism of riots, apparently considered that study
reports did not sell newspapers. According to Clifford, "the
reaction of the press was 'so what. . . it only has to do with
prisons'."(92) Don Clifford continued, "there was no interest
from the press prior to the riot at Attica. . . it only stirred
interest after the fact of the Attica riot."(93)

As noted in the Greenberg report, Oswald tried to change
the Department from a custodial orientation to one emphasizing
rehabilitation. He actively tried to recruit Black and Puerto
Rican correctional officers by sending recruiters and job
interviewers to New York City and other urban areas and even
contacted the Governor of Puerto Rico regarding the employment
possibilities with New York State Corrections.(94) He
discontinued the censorship of mail, while the cases were still
being tried in the federal courts. He gave the inmate free access
to the telephone at the inmate's expense and tried to recruit

volunteers to inaugurate evening programs in order to reduce evening cell time. He extended the furlough and work release programs and started law libraries in each of the institutions. He ordered the food to be upgraded to meet nutritional standards as set by the Federal Government, no matter what the cost.(95) And as noted in other public documents, Oswald's first reforms were in procedures already under attack in the courts:

> he granted mail and visiting privileges to inmates' common-law spouses; revised censorship procedures to permit inmates to correspond privately with attorneys and public officials; and allowed greater accessibility of news media to prisons to increase public knowledge of conditions.(96)

As Oswald has stated, in all of these reforms he received no assistance from the traditional religious/social reformers and incurred the hostility of the correctional officers who were fearful of inmates out of their cells.(97) Thus Oswald was compelled to initiate some of the aforementioned changes with the use of federal funds.(98) But it must be noted, as demonstrated, that the legislature, the executive, and the religious/social reformers did not come to Oswald's assistance in his attempt to initiate reform programs intended to be beneficial to inmate interests. At the same time, custodial interests incurred no loss of funding or job positions. Tense conditions continued within the prisons, increasingly so within the state prisons which now housed rebellious inmates previously involved in the New York City jail riots and the Auburn riot.

On September 9, 1971, violence erupted at the maximum security prison in Attica, New York.(99) A discussion of this riot and its aftermath will serve to indicate conflicting interests in the New York State correctional system and governmental response to those interests.

Attica State Prison Riot

At the time of the inmate rebellion, Attica housed more than 2,000 inmates (54.9% Black, 37.7% White and 6.9% Puerto Rican, .05% other).(100) Much controversy would later develop as to whether the riot was spontaneous or planned. This would seem to be a moot issue for according to Commissioner Russell G. Oswald,

> the rebels armed in advance with knives,

92

> spears, clubs, swords, steel and metal
> pipes, pickaxes, shovels, straight razors,
> wire bolos and baseball bats with
> extended spikes took. . . control of A,
> B, D and E Blocks within twenty minutes.
> Then the rebels attacked the commissary,
> metal shops, industrial buildings and set
> fires in the auditorium, chapel and school
> house. . . . After a sharp struggle, the
> rebels took C Block. They had won
> control of most of the maximum security
> institution within thirty minutes.(101)

The only areas that remained in the control of the administration
were the Administration Building, Housing Block Z, the hospital,
mess hall, powerhouse, the vehicles and the perimeter wall.(102)

Several guards were seriously injured in the take-over by
the inmates; one was later to die of wounds inflicted by the
inmates. In all, inmates held thirty-nine hostages, some of whom
were guards; others, civilian employees.

Mancusi, the Superintendent of Attica, with the assistance
of the State Police and other correction officers, soon regained
control of E, A and C Blocks. According to observers, many of
the inmates had remained in their cells declaring that they wanted
no part of the rebellion and adding that the militants were "wild
men, crazy radicals, who had been planning the thing for weeks,
threatening to kill any inmate who informed on them."(103)
Control was soon restored over 962 of the inmates.(104)

However, more than 1,200 inmates were still in control of
the hostages and B and D Blocks and the recreational yards
which intersected at the point known as Times Square. The
confrontation was now no longer just between guards and inmates,
for each group had immediately drawn to its side various other
interests who were to clash during the riot and after.

Rallying to the support of the correction officers who
wanted immediately to go in with force and regain control of the
institution(105) and the hostages were "more than 500 State
Police, 250 sheriffs' deputies, and more than 250 correction
officers."(106) Later, national guardsmen would be added to this
contingent. But Oswald decided, against the advice of his staff,
to negotiate with the prisoners for the peaceful release of the
hostages. This brought much vituperation upon him by the
correctional officers. According to Oswald,

> from several correctional officers. . . . I
> received such treatment as I have never

93

before experienced in my career. Often
when I passed by, they would utter
curses, epithets and obscenities. . . .
They were made to me and at me, as I
passed by.(107)

In other prisons, many correction officers worked up petitions
calling for Oswald's resignation and at least one was sent to the
Governor. At another prison, a group of correction officers
drafted a petition signed by the individual officers asking the FBI
to come in and rescue them if they were ever taken hostage in a
prison riot. In the petition was a requirement that neither
Oswald nor Dunbar (Deputy Commissioner) was to be permitted to
intervene. The petition continued, "these two men, with their
policies and programs have left a sickening number of dead
correctional personnel from coast to coast."(108)

And thus while McGinnis was always identified by the
correction officers as "one of us", Oswald was viewed as an
outsider, a social worker and do-gooder who was pandering to
criminals.(109) Previously, bureaucratic and administration policy
were the same within the Correction Department, namely an
overriding commitment to security and custody; however, now
the administration was supporting a policy of rehabilitation and
the bureaucracy was adamant in a firm commitment to custody and
security. Now, administration and bureaucratic policy diverged
and this was a constant source of conflict within the Department
of Correctional Services.

Relations between Oswald and the correctional officers were
further exacerbated by Oswald's acceptance of the inmates' list of
twenty-eight demands presented below. This list of demands is
presented in its entirety to indicate that despite the revolutionary
rhetoric that accompanied the demands, the demands represent a
rather basic, humane reordering of the prison along the lines
traditionally espoused by the early twentieth century reformers,
as described in Chapter one of this work. The Governor had
also telephoned approval of these demands in order to secure the
safe release of the hostages.(110) The demands were as follows:

1) Provide adequate food, water and shelter for all
inmates.
2) Inmates shall be permitted to return to their
cells. . . under their own power.
3) Grant complete administrative amnesty to all
persons associated with this matter. By
administrative amnesty, the state agreed not to take
any adverse parole actions, administrative
proceedings, physical punishment or other type of
harassment, segregating any inmates or keeping them

in isolation or lock-up.

4) Recommend the application of the New York State minimum wage law standards to all work done by inmates.

5) Establish by October 1, 1971 a permanent ombudsman service for the facility staffed by appropriate persons from the neighboring communities.

6) Allow all New York State prisoners to be politically active without intimidation or reprisal.

7) Allow true religious freedom.

8) End all censorship of newspapers, magazines, and other publications from publishers unless there is determined by qualified authority which includes the ombudsman that literature in question presents a clear and present danger to the safety and security of the institution. Institution spot censoring only of letters.

9) Allow all inmates at their own expense to communicate with any one they please.

10) Institute realistic, effective rehabilitation programs for all inmates according to their offense and personal needs.

11) Modernize the inmate education system, including establishment of a Latin library.

12) Provide or allow adequate legal assistance to all inmates requesting it or permit them to use inmate legal assistants of their choice - in any proceeding whatsoever.

13) Provide an effective narcotics treatment program for all prisoners requesting such treatment.

14) Reduce cell time, increase recreation time, and provide better recreation facilities and equipment, hopefully by November 1, 1971.

15) Provide a healthy diet; reduce the number of pork dishes; increase fresh fruit daily.

16) Provide adequate medical treatment for every inmate; engage either a Spanish-speaking Doctor or inmate interpreter who will accompany Spanish-speaking inmates to medical interviews.

17) Institute a program for the recruitment and employment of a significant number of Black and Spanish-speaking officers.

18) Establish an inmate grievance commission, comprised of one elected inmate from each company, which is authorized to speak to the administration concerning grievances and develop other procedures for inmate participation in the operation and decision-making processes of the institution.

19) Investigate the alleged expropriation of inmate funds and the use of profits from the metal and other

95

shops.

20) The State Commissioner of Correctional Services will recommend that the Penal Law be changed to cease administrative resentencing of inmates returned for parole violations.

21) Recommend that Menenchino hearings be held promptly and fairly. (Menenchino parole decisions held in general that parolees were entitled to counsel in violation hearings.)

22) Recommend necessary legislation and more adequate funds to expand work release programs.

23) End approved lists for correspondence and visitors.

24) Remove visitation screens as soon as possible. (This had been recommended by Senator John R. Dunne in May 1970 at public hearings in New York City on Family Visits; but, no administrative change had been forthcoming by McGinnis.)

25) Institute a thirty-day maximum for segregation arising out of any one offense.

26) Paroled inmates shall not be charged with parole violations for moving traffic violations or for driving without a license, unconnected with any other crime.

27) Permit access to outside dentists and doctors at the inmate's own expense within the institution, where possible and consistent with scheduling problems, medical diagnosis and health needs.

28) It is expressly understood that members of the Observer Committee will be permitted into the institution on a reasonable basis to determine whether all of the above provisions are being effectively carried out.(111)

The formation of an "observer committee", composed of individuals requested by the inmates and others and who were to act as a negotiating team between the rebelling inmates and the correctional administration was another source of discontent for the correctional officers since they perceived the Observer Committee as another concession to inmate demands. In fact, the Observer Committee, which comprised some members of radical organizations as well as legislators, newsmen and others, viewed themselves as a neutral body.(112) But in this instance, as in others throughout the negotiations, the correction officers felt that the inmates were being accorded very favorable treatment at the risk of the lives of fellow correction officers being held hostage.

Oswald had accepted the twenty-eight demands and as he stated, "I felt that most of the twenty-eight demands were reasonable and the rest were part of the price we would pay to save thirty-eight hostages."(113)

But the inmate demands escalated, partially due to the death of one of the correction officers, which by state law mandated the death penalty for those judged guilty of his death. At this point, inmate demands escalated to include transportation to a non-imperialist country, removal of Superintendent Mancusi, and complete criminal amnesty. The Governor refused to consider the issue of criminal amnesty;(114) negotiations broke down and the State Police were given the command to enter the yard and free the hostages.

In the aftermath of the take-over in which eleven hostages and thirty inmates were killed, all by gunshots from the state police or other members of the rescue team,(115) Oswald was again blamed by the custodial interests for the deaths of the hostages because he had negotiated and waited too long in retaking the prison. He or the Governor was also held responsible for the deaths of the inmates by other inmates, Black and Puerto Rican minorities outside the prison, and by radical "New Left" groups not previously involved in penal matters, because of the excessive force used by attacking troopers and police. However, in many of the demonstrations that followed, the Governor and not Oswald was castigated by the radical groups for the deaths.

Immediately after the riot, both the guards and inmates secured some of their demands, the nature of which will be discussed below. It should be noted that inmate demands, although essentially rehabilitative in nature, were not the result of an alliance with the religious /social reformers.

Correctional officers threatened a mass demonstration during which officers would "lock-in" prisoners, feeding them, but otherwise not letting them out of their cells, unless the Correction Department and the Governor agreed to their demands. The correction officers, through their union spokesman, demanded that "the six to ten percent of incorrigible prisoners be segregated from inmates who could be rehabilitated; that guards be trained better and prisons equipped with better communications systems."(116) The correction officers' union spokesman stated, "we're regretful we have to take this strong stand but. . . the lock-in will continue as long as it takes."(117) And as a result, both Commissioner Oswald and Governor Rockefeller acquiesced to the demands for a separate institution for incorrigible prisoners. In popular jargon, the institution became known as the "maxi-maxi" prison; that is, a maximum security section within a maximum security prison institution.

And although this demand for the "maxi-maxi" was

specifically a demand of the correction officers, other members of the bureaucracy likewise supported the proposal. The Catholic Chaplain at Elmira had stated, "major prison upheavals are going to recur in New York State unless a separate institution is opened for about one hundred and fifty hard core militant Marxist revolutionaries, as tight as Alcatraz used to be."(118) The Chaplain's additional comments indicated the inherent conflict between the custodial interests and all other reformers. The Chaplain scoffed at the

> instant experts who are calling for
> reforms based on a vacuum of first hand
> knowledge. A man cannot be helped
> against his will. . . the eggheads do not
> understand this because they do not know
> prison nature.(119)

Russell G. Oswald was forced to accede to the demands for the "maxi-maxi" by threats to rebel and close down the prison system, not by the inmates, but by the correction officers and superintendents of the various institutions. And the Governor responded to many of the demands of the correctional officers, even though not all of their demands were met.

In the fiscal appropriations distributed after the Attica riot, the correctional officer/custodial interests received an overwhelming proportion of the monies. In the Governor's Executive Budget of 1972- 1973, presented in the months after Attica, an increase of almost ten million dollars was allocated to the Department of Correctional Services for state operating expenses. All but one million was allocated for new correctional officer positions, salary increases, farm and plant maintenance and renovation of Attica Prison. Four million in capital construction expenses, which were part of the capital construction budget and not the state operating budget, was allocated for the refurbishing of existing buildings, increased security, showers for the inmates and a new gym at Elmira. Funds were also included for the conversion of part of one of the maximum security institutions into the so-called "maxi-maxi" prison.(120)

But even though initial funds were assigned to the creation of the "maxi-maxi" prison, this demand of the correction officers, agreed to by Oswald after a meeting with union officials in October of 1971,(121) was not without opposition. It was opposed by inmate organizations such as the Fortune Society, and also by some legislators present at Attica during the riot, notably, Arthur Eve, a Democratic liberal Assemblyman from Buffalo, and John R. Dunne, a moderate Republican from Long Island. (122) Dunne was vociferously opposed to the establishment of such an institution on the grounds that it would be characterized "as a black concentration camp that might be more destructive than those forces which we are trying now to overcome."(123) It must be noted that there is again no record of the involvement of the religious/social reformers either for or against the institution of a "maxi-maxi".

The original appropriation of $1.3 million presented in an early draft of the Governor's proposed supplemental budget for the "special treatment facility for radical, militant, recalcitrant, and dangerous inmates" was deleted early in May of 1972 due to "protests by several legislators, among them Robert Garcia (Democratic Senator from the Bronx, subsequently elected to Congress) and John Dunne who complained that they believed such a 'maxi-maxi' prison would be used as a vehicle to punish inmates who engaged in political activity." (124)   Instead, according to Rockefeller's Budget Director, Richard Dunham, "funds that would have been used for the 'maxi-maxi' would be spent to intensify correctional services at existing maximum security facilities." (125) And according to the Senate Finance Majority staff,

> the consensus of people very interested in the corrections problem was that one 'maxi-maxi' institution was not the way to go. . . the only difference is this: instead of having one unit as such, there is money provided for having units at each prison. (126)

Thus in reality the correctional officers secured several tangible benefits by way of additional staff, more secure facilities, riot equipment, and an intensified training course. The defeat of the "maxi-maxi" was in many ways only a symbolic defeat, for the money allocated was merely redistributed in the interests of the custodial interests, namely toward increased security at all of the maximum security prisons.   Had the money been reallocated toward rehabilitative interests, the correctional interests would have suffered a very real defeat.   But this was not the case.

As noted above, the defeat of the "maxi-maxi" was credited to Legislative opposition.   Again the religious/social reformers remained silent.   They were obviously not a force opposed to the demands of the correction officers for such a facility.   But other interests may have played a role in the defeat of the correction officers' primary demand.   The possibility that the courts might rule that such a facility was unconstitutional was no doubt also a consideration.   But the interest to be examined is one of the pro-correctional officers interests, namely, the demands of their union, Council 82 of the American Federation of State County Municipal Employees (AFSCME).

It is interesting to note that after the Auburn riot and also after the Attica riot, correction officers' demands included prison reform proposals identical to that of the inmate demands. According to one observer, Council 82's broader membership might explain why penal reform measures were included along with demands for increased security. (127) According to this observer, the National President (Jerry Wurf) of the AFSCME, a union which included many low income Blacks and whose leadership desired a liberal image, (128) was also union spokesman for the correction officers whose main interests were in security. In trying to satisfy both of the groups he represented, Wurf is quoted as saying that the guards did not want repression and "unless the inmates are treated in a reasonable manner," the prison system would not be secure. (129) Wurf therefore endorsed prisoner demands for more showers and better sanitation facilities; "this business of toilet paper every three weeks, one shower a week and bad clothing does not contribute to a reasonable environment." (130)

Thus, Wurf advocated maintenance of the status quo rewards for the guards plus such reforms as had been instituted by Oswald, justifying these reforms as maintaining custodial control. The guards themselves might not have supported even such minor reforms; one official noted that guards throughout the state were calling for the ouster of Oswald "who backs prison reform,"(131) since they saw these reforms as endangering the custodial security of the prisons. But it might also be noted that such reforms could be instituted without endangering the substantive rewards such as jobs and money to the guards since the reforms demanded neither massive investments of funds nor overall policy change. Thus the union which represented the guards as a sub-group sought to satisfy the interests of the guards while advocating reforms to satisfy its wider membership.

Reform measures were given wide publicity in the press, at mass demonstrations and by the various study commissions set up to study the situation that had sparked the Attica riot. And the reformers who took to the streets to protest prison conditions were not the older religious/social reformers, but the militant activists who had gained experience in the Vietnam War protests.

Immediately after Attica, a mass rally was held in New York City to protest the Attica Prison massacre which was compared to My Lai. Sponsoring the rally, which was attended by three hundred protesters, were the Ad Hoc Committee to Protest the Attica Massacre, Vietnam Veterans Against the War, the War Resisters' League, the Harrisburg Defense Committee and others identified with the anti-war movement.(132) A Concerned Clergy on Attica group was also formed, requesting to monitor Attica cell blocks to prevent reprisals and beatings by the guards.(133)

And other clergy groups, including a large segment of the New York City Black clergymen and the New York Clergy Coalition, based in New York City, held services of mourning for the inmates and angrily denounced the Governor's handling of the prison riot. Charges of genocide against Blacks and poor Whites were leveled against the state by these clergy groups only recently active in minority rights and penal reform.(134)

The older, more traditional religious/social reformers were not visible, even though later some members did become involved in the work of the legislative study commissions and the investigatory studies established after the Attica riot. Russell G. Oswald noted their absence while stating that "on the whole, I initiated reforms alone, with no assistance from the reformers."(135) And Senator John R. Dunne had also noted the absence of the religious/social reformers in his attempts at reform.(136) Vito Ternullo, former Director of the Division of Education in the Department of Correction, has stated that, "aside from the Quakers, no religious group had become significantly active in corrections until the Muslims."(137) Consequently there was very little organized support, aside from inmate interests, for reform measures in the Governor's Budget of 1972-1973.

As noted in Newsday, January 21, 1972, although Governor Rockefeller's budget proposals were accompanied by a call for prison reform, the dollar figures he sent to the Legislature indicated that almost all of the new money was allocated for increased security and administration.(138)

> Some programs generally associated with reform. . . may even receive less money in the 1972-1973 budget than this year. Among the reform measures proposed by the Governor, but not funded in his budget, are more minimum security facilities, widespread use of temporary releases for work, training or family visits, increased education and training and halfway houses for parolees. In addition, federal aid, which might be used to promote such reforms often is used instead as a budget balancing tool. Because a federal grant, for instance, will supply $403,000 for inmate clothing, the state has deducted exactly that amount from its own budget. . . . A spokesman for the Correction Department conceded in Albany that there is little or no money in the proposed budget for the

Governor's proposed reforms. (139)

In the aftermath of Attica, the Governor stated again and again his concern for Corrections. But in the budget initially presented by Oswald to the Governor's budget staff, $22 million in proposed funds were cut - most of them in the area of rehabilitative programming. (140) As noted in "closed door" legislative budget hearings, (141) cut from Oswald's proposed budget by the Budget Division staff were: $3 million for counseling and classification; $1.2 million for educational, vocational, physical education and recreational program staff and additional funds for volunteer services, narcotic programs and administrative and religious activities involving the participation of Black and Spanish-speaking clergymen. (142) An additional allocation of $3 million was cut in custodial areas; but the greatest percentage of a cut was that given to the rehabilitative programs, according to Commissioner Oswald. (143) When asked why the priority was given to custodial positions and not rehabilitative positions, Oswald responded, "we can get the money for custodial positions more readily." (144)

In his testimony before the Legislative Budget hearing, Oswald stated,

> I am fully cognizant that at the time this Executive Budget was prepared, the Governor and his administration faced one of the worst fiscal crises in the state's history. If it had not been for this crucial fiscal problem, I am fully confident that the Governor would have incorporated in his budget request. . . sufficient appropriations which would permit this Department to adjust the post-adjudicative system toward greater treatment orientation than is possible under present circumstances. (145)

Commissioner Oswald continued,

> the budget freeze has taken a heavy toll in our efforts to upgrade the correctional system. . . I want to emphasize that the present level of appropriations will not be sufficient to enable this Department to achieve what many public officials and the public at large, the courts and all pressure groups request and demand. . . . (146)

But it must be noted that even prior to the Taxpayers' Revolt, requests of $9 million for forestry camps for adult inmates, a medium security treatment modality, had been cut by the Governor's budget staff in the 1971-1972 budget.(147)   Thus, in many instances, there seems to have been little support within the Executive branch of state government for the rehabilitative concepts espoused by Oswald.

The budget as presented by the Governor's budget staff (Division of the Budget) also received tacit support from the Legislative Finance Committees since they had the power to make changes in that budget but neglected to do so.   When Oswald attempted to justify his original Budget proposal and obtain the program and staff allocations which had been cut by the budget staff of the Governor, the Chairman of the Assembly Ways and Means Committee hastened to cut off this line of questioning with the remark, "these are details that can be cleared up later.   We can clear this all up."(148) Legislative leaders seemed extremely hesitant to challenge Gubernatorial budget determinations in the correctional arena.(149)

Russell G. Oswald has summarized the fiscal state of the Correctional Services Department.   "There has been a definite diminution of percentage of state funds given to the Department of Correction each year from 1966 right down through 1971 and the Department has a lesser percentage of the total state dollar. . . each year it becomes less."(150)   Consequently, "corrections has had to seek monies from the federal government in areas that are traditionally state responsibility including personnel, fiscal planning, program evaluation and food and clothing."(151)

And Oswald has stated that even after the Attica revolt, he still could not get money for programs because of a polarization in the Legislature between the pro-inmate interests and those who supported custodial interests.(152) One legislator in Oswald's corner was Democratic Assemblyman, Stanley Steingut.   Oswald has noted that in a meeting after Attica, Steingut stated "Commissioner why didn't you come to me?   We would have helped you with increased funding."(153) But as Oswald noted, "we couldn't go to members of another party, the Governor would not have tolerated that."(154)

By March of 1972, five months after Attica, Oswald stated that the following steps had been taken: a total of 339 new corrections officers had been recruited and 273 of them had been assigned to jobs;   thousands of gas masks and helmets had been distributed to the prison institutions and bidding would soon begin on "new and diversified" metal detectors.   Inmate improvements included better nutritional standards, an increase in

103

the number of showers allowed prisoners and the establishment of inmate liaison committees, an expanded clothing issue and a better provision of toilet paper. (155)

While it might appear as if tangible benefits were accorded inmates, it must be noted again that they did not involve large expenditures of money nor fundamental policy changes within the system. In other words, these changes did not move the prison system away from custody and towards rehabilitation and hence were merely ameliorations within the present structure. Therefore, the correctional officers received tangible benefits from governmental officials while the inmates received benefits which strictly speaking perhaps might be considered tangible, but were very different in nature from those received by the correctional bureaucracy. This difference will be discussed in the conclusion.

And in the wake of the Attica revolt, various study commissions were set up to investigate the causes of the riot. Like so many of the study commissions before this one, a basic rehabilitative bias was obvious. The most notable study commission was the New York State Special Commission on Attica, informally known as the McKay Commission, after its Director, Robert McKay, Dean of the New York University Law School. In general, the Commission suggested that the New York State prison system should be restructured using the following principles as guidelines:

> 1) If prisoners are to learn to bear the responsibilities of citizens, they must have all the rights of other citizens, except that. . . of liberty of person. . . .
> 2) The confinement associated with the deprivation of liberty of person should be the least that is administratively necessary. . . .
> 3) The programs and policies associated with confinement should be directed at elevating and enhancing the dignity, worth, and self confidence of the inmates, not at debasing and dehumanizing them. . . .
> 4). . . Community groups and outside professionals should be allowed and encouraged to participate regularly in the life of each correctional facility. . . .
> 5) Training for correction officers must sensitize them to understand and deal with the new breed of young inmates from the urban ghettos and to understand and control the racism within themselves. Correctional facilities must be staffed by persons motivated to help inmates. . . .

104

6) Vocational training and other educational programs should be conducted in accordance with the preceding principles. . . .
7) For a correctional system to satisfy the principles here enunciated, the grant or denial of parole must be measured by clear and comprehensive standards, disseminated to inmates in advance. . . . (156)

But more important than its recommendations, which were rehabilitative in mode, was the fact that the study commission, perceived as a "whitewash" by inmate groups did in fact criticize the Governor's actions regarding the Attica rebellion. The McKay Commision stated that the Governor was wrong in deciding not to go to Attica. The Commission stated,

> the Governor should have gone to Attica. . . because his responsibilities as the state's chief executive made it appropriate that he be present at the scene of the critical decision (the ordering of the armed assault on rebel inmates) involving great risk of loss of life after the Commissioner, Russell Oswald had requested him to come. (157)

The McKay Commission thus affirmed itself to be sympathetic to the inmates and liberal reformers. However, these groups lacked power and almost de facto the McKay Commission study has been relegated to dusty library shelves instead of forming the basis of an action program endorsed by the bureaucratic and political powers.

After the Attica revolt, some legislative concessions were made to the inmate group. In May of 1972, the Governor signed into law bills which permitted : ex-convicts to work in supermarkets where alcoholic beverages were sold; allowed ex-convicts convicted of only one felony to be exempted from all restrictions on employment; and two bills which removed what the Governor called a "glaring injustice" in the law by making all persons convicted of comparable crimes eligible for parole after serving the same time, whether or not they were convicted before the Penal Law was changed in 1967. (158) This bill was originally introduced in the 1968 session of the Legislature. Again none of these measures involved large expenditures of money nor fundamental policy changes. The legislative proposals generally affected the status of inmates once released from the prison system and therefore were not in strict opposition to custodial interests. Thus general legislative and reform apathy continued into subsequent legislative sessions as the following discussion of legislative proposals will indicate.

In January of 1973, Community Service Society's Committee on Youth and Correction, called for the adoption of a bill of rights for prisoners, which would guarantee

> . . . the right to freedom of expression, to the exercise of religion, to receive mail, newspapers, or literature without restriction, to receive open-contact visits. . . the right to adequate clothing, medical assistance and care commensurate with human dignity. . . the right to due process in any disciplinary proceeding, to institute suit or legal proceedings, to the franchise in accordance with the regulations governing absentee ballots.(159)

It should be noted that court decisions had previously expanded inmate rights in many of the areas mentioned above. But in the era after Attica, "prisoner rights" became a catch phrase used by the religious/ social reformers in an attempt supposedly to identify with the civil libertarians whose arena was not the legislature but the courts and where some success had been achieved in this area of prisoner rights.

Other measures supported by the Community Service Society were: new and diversified correctional facilities; removal of the employment disabilities for ex-offenders; expanded training and employment opportunities for inmates and correctional personnel; revitalization of the State Commission of Correction (a watchdog agency in name only since the Commissioner of the Department of Correction was simultaneously the Director of the State Commission of Correction); removal of superintendents of correctional facilities from the civil service competitive class.(160)

Community Service Society was supported by other reform groups on many of the aforementioned issues. The removal of job disabilities for ex-offenders was in general supported by the Legal Aid, Correctional Association of New York, New York Urban Coalition, League of Women Voters, New York State Council of Churches and the New York Civil Liberties Union. These same groups supported expansion of furlough and visitor privileges; abolition of censorship of mail; institution of basic due process in prison disciplinary proceedings; equalization of sentencing between the old and new Penal Law. In addition, the reform groups "strongly urged that the $16 million for treatment programs requested by the Department of Correctional Services, and dropped from the 1973-74 Executive Budget, be reinstated in the supplemental budget."(161)

It is interesting to note that although Connery and Benjamin claim that Rockefeller exempted the Department of Correctional Services (DOCS) from expenditure restrictions placed on all other state agencies in the 1973-1974 fiscal year and further that "Rockefeller proposed an additional $12 million for the DOCS, $1.3 million to be spent for a 'maximum program, maximum security' facility requested by the Department and the rest for additional personnel and the upgrading of prison services,"(162) this amount ($16 million) and more was dropped from the budget by the Governor's own Division of the Budget.

But reform interests generally were not successful. The package of prisoner rights proposals was "killed" in the Legislature as well as the bills that sought to liberalize an inmate's standing in areas of citizenship, medical and dental care, and parole and disciplinary areas.(163) The proposals which were passed reduced by $15 million the prison capital construction program, thus eliminating four of six proposed minimum security community centers for prisoners nearing release. The only measure which passed by way of reform was a bill which allowed a prisoner to visit the deathbed of a guardian.(164)

As Polly Feingold, legislative representative of the New York Urban Coalition, summed up

> as memories of Attica recede, the urgency of changing the criminal justice system diminishes - or at least is refocused from reform to repression. For example, thirteen prison reform bills. . . which had the support of citizens' organizations across the state, generally did not even get reported out of their respective committees.(165)

The rationale given, according to Ms. Feingold, was that the new Commissioner of the Correctional Services Department, Peter Preiser, who was appointed by the Governor upon Russell Oswald's resignation in April of 1973, should be given the opportunity to effect the changes described in the bills administratively, rather than saddling him with legislative requirements. A similar rationale was used to avoid legislative action, according to Ms. Feingold, on reforms promised by Oswald to the Attica inmates in September of 1971, that is, it would be preferable to have these reforms effected administratively rather than legislatively.(166) This course of action, of course, freed the correctional bureaucracy from outside mandates, thus permitting it to follow its traditional policy of absolute control.

107

In fact, Oswald would have needed legislative support to effect administrative change since he did not have the support of the correctional bureaucracy. Perhaps this was one of the reasons why Oswald resigned in the early part of 1973. Upon his resignation in April of 1973, Governor Rockefeller appointed Peter Preiser, who had been serving as the state's Director of Probation and may be remembered from Chapter three as the Executive Director of the 1965 Governor's Special Committee on Criminal Offenders, as the new Commissioner of the Department of Correctional Services. Oswald was virtually removed from the criminal justice arena by his Gubernatorial appointment to a position on the Crime Victims Compensation Board.

By this time also, Senator John Dunne was no longer serving as Chairman of the Senate Committee on Crime and Correction, having been appointed to the chairmanship of the Senate Insurance Committee. Dunne had incurred the wrath of Governor Rockefeller when after the Attica riot, he had attempted to conduct his own investigation of penal conditions.(167) The new Chairman of the Senate Committee on Crime and Correction was Ralph Marino, a conservative Republican from Long Island who had evidenced no prior involvement or interest in the criminal justice field.(168)

And in June of 1973, another group appointed by Rockefeller after Attica and known as the Select Committee on Correctional Institutions and Program, noted that the state's prisons had made

> some progress since Attica, but that change, which has a fundamental impact on the day to day existence of the inmate population remains elusive. . . . The prison system in general and Attica in particular, continues to be plagued by a lack of budget money, legislative indifference, poor morale and incidents of violence.(169)

Mr. Richard Bartlett, Chairman of the Select Committee in 1973, stated that budgetary tightening had forced cancellation of education programs for functionally illiterate inmates; efforts to decrease the number of cell hours had failed because there was no money to pay the guards the overtime that would accompany such a plan.(170) He continued to state that one of the major recommendations of the Select Committee, that the Correctional Services Department plan and build community based small prisons, was cut drastically by the Legislative fiscal committees who reduced the request for twelve of these to two. (171) In addition, the report of the Select Committee stated that there were "frequent reports of poor morale within the Department of Correctional Services and a disquieting level of violence and assaultive behavior among inmates."(172)

Among the improvements noted by Bartlett, were an attempt to expand work release programs, an effort to classify inmates according to rehabilitative needs and more liaison committees between inmates and prison authorities; also, some minority members had been recruited as guards; inmates had received small pay raises; visiting facilities had been improved and the system had moved to a nutritional rather than economic food standard.(173) But many of the above "improvements" had been initiated by Oswald two years previously.(174) In general, it may be stated that the system had remained fundamentally the same.

Thus, it is evident that the political commitment to prison reform had begun to wane even before the ink had dried on the final reports of the study commissions. Connery and Benjamin have noted that Rockefeller had learned, as had Franklin Delano Roosevelt before him, that "in the scramble for state funds, the legislature placed budgetary requests of the Correction Department far below state aid to local school districts, which had a much greater impact on their chances for re-election."(175)

And yet there is sufficient evidence to show that the legislature was not solely to blame for inadequate funding of Corrections, some blame must also be shared as well by the Governor and his executive staff. The dictum "there are no votes in prisons" applies to the executive as well as to the legislature. Because the inmates constituted no one's political constituency, the benefits they were to reap were small.

In the realm of real politics and popular interests, prison conditions and policies continued to have a low priority despite lip service to their importance.

Endnotes-Chapter IV

1. See chapter three, p. 51.

2. Ibid., p. 56.

3. The Official Report of the New York State Special Commission on Attica (New York: Bantam Books, 1972), p. 116.

4. Ibid., pp. 114-116.

5. Ibid., pp. 117-118.

6. Ibid., p. 118.

7. Ibid., See also, Ben M. Crouch, Editor The Keepers (Springfield, Ill.: Charles C. Thomas, 1980) pp. 20-24. and Charles Stastny and Gabrielle Tyrnauer Who Rules the Joint? (Lexington, MA: D.C. Heath and Co., 1982) pp. 143-145 re: the Washington State Penitentiary at Walla Walla.

8. The Official Report of the New York State Special Commission on Attica, pp. 116-117.

9. Jessica Mitford, "Kind and Usual Punishment in California" in Prisons, Protest and Politics, ed. Burton Atkins and Henry Glick, (Englewood Cliffs, N.J.: Prentice Hall Inc., 1972) pp. 163-64.

10. Bethea v. Crouse 417 F2d (10th Cir. 1969) in William Bennett Turner, "Establishing the Rule of Law in Prisons: A Manual for Prisoners' Rights Litigation", in Marilyn Haft and Michele Herman, Prisoners' Rights, vol.1 (New York: Practicing Law Institute, 1972), pp. 69-114, esp. p.69, footnote 2.

11. Interview with Russell Oswald, former Commissioner of the Department of Correctional Services, March 19, 1975.

12. Inmates of Cook County Jail v. Tierney (No. 68C 504 ND 111 August 22, 1968) in William Turner, "Establishing the Rule of Law in Prisons" in Haft and Herman, Prisoners' Rights, p. 72

13. Turner, "Establishing the Rule of Law in Prisons" in Haft and Herman, Prisoners' Rights, p. 74.

14. Ibid.

15. Ibid., p. 77

16.   Ibid.,: see Fortune Society v. McGinnis 319 F Supp 901 (SDNY 1970), p. 82; Carothers v. Follette 314 F Supp 1014 (SDNY 1970), p. 83; Candelaria v. Mancusi (Civil No. 1970-491 WDNY Jan. 7, 1971) p. 83.

17.   Michael Milleman, "Prison Disciplinary Hearings and Procedural Due Process - the Requirement of a Full Administrative Hearing", in Haft and Herman, Prisoners' Rights, 2: 149-181, esp. p. 150.

18.   Turner, "Establishing the Rule of Law in Prisons", p. 80.

19.   Ibid.

20.   Milleman, "Prison Disciplinary Hearings and Procedural Due Process" pp. 150-151.

21.   Ibid.

22.   Sostre v. Rockefeller (312 F Supp 872 SDNY 1970) in Milleman, "Prison Disciplinary Hearings and Procedural Due Process", p. 152, footnote 2.

23.   Sostre v. McGinnis (No. 35038 2nd Cir. Feb. 24, 1971) in Milleman, "Prison Disciplinary Hearings and Procedural Due Process", p. 153.

24.   Ibid. New York Times, 25 February 1971, pp. 1, 52.

25.   Sostre v. McGinnis in Milleman, "Prison Disciplinary Hearings and Procedural Due Process", p. 153, footnote 29.

26.   Milleman, "Prison Disciplinary Hearings and Procedural Due Process" p. 153.

27.   Interview with Vito Ternullo, former Director of the Division of Education in the Department of Correction, May 9, 1974.

28.   Interview with Russell G. Oswald, March 19, 1975.

29.   The Official Report of the New York State Special Commission on Attica,   p. 125.

30.   Russell G. Oswald Attica My Story (Garden City: Doubleday & Co., 1972) p. 209.

31.   Daily News, 18 August 1970, p. 3.

32.   New York Times, 19 August 1970, p. 22.

33. Daily News, 19 August 1970, p. 4.

34. Ibid.

35. New York Times, 8 October 1970, p. 37.

36. Daily News, 20 August 1970, p. 6.

37. Sunday News, 4 October 1970, p. 7.

38. Atkins and Glick, Prisons Protest and Politics, Introduction, p. 6.

39. Ibid.

40. New York Times, 19 August 1970, p. 22.

41. Barbara Lavin, Participant Observer, September 1967-May 1970.

42. Ibid.

43. Interview with John R. Dunne, March 17, 1975.

44. Daily News, 18 August 1970, p. 3.

45. Daily News, 19 September 1970, p. 22.

46. Ibid. This Associated Press Release likewise appeared in the September 19, 1970 issue of the Buffalo Evening News and The Schenectady Gazette, among others.

47. See Chapter one.

48. Atkins and Glick, Prisons, Protest and Politics, Introduction p. 2

49. New York Times, 8 October 1970, p. 37.

50. Ibid.

51. Ibid.

52. Ibid.

53. Christian Science Monitor, 19 December 1970, p. 3.

54. Atkins and Glick, Prisons, Protest and Politics, Introduction, p. 8.

55. Michael Lipsky, "Protest as a Political Resource", American Political Science Review 62 (December 1968): 1144-1158, as quoted in Atkins and Glick, Prisons, Protest and Politics, pp. 4-5.

56. New York Times, 8 October 1970, p. 37.

57. New York Times, 19 August 1970, p. 22 and New York Times, 21 August 1970, p. 30.

58. New York Times, 3 September 1970.

59. New York Times, 12 October 1971, p. 29.

60. New York Times, 5 November 1970, p. 54.

61. Long Island Press, 2 February 1971.

62. Daily News, 15 August 1970, p. 3.

63. Syracuse Post Standard, 5 November 1970, p. 3.

64. Ibid.

65. New York Times, 11 February 1971.

66. New York Times, 17 May 1971, p. 37.

67. Citizen Advertiser, Auburn, New York, 26 March 1971, p. 10.

68. New York Times, 17 May 1971, pp. 37 and 44.

69. New York Times, 17 May 1971, p. 37.

70. New York Times, 17 May 1971, pp. 37 and 44.

71. Interview with Vito Ternullo, May 9, 1974.

72. Ibid.

73. Ibid.

74. Testimony of Russell G. Oswald before the New York State Special Commission on Attica. Public Hearings broadcasted over Channel 13 WNET, April 28, 1972. Personal tape recording.

75. Interview with Walter Dunbar, Deputy Commissioner of the Department of Correctional Services under Russell Oswald, May 29, 1974.

76.   The Official Report of the New York State Special Commission on Attica, p. 131.

77.   Interview with Frances Kernohan, staff associate for Community Service Society's Youth and Correction Committee, March 3, 1975.

78.   Testimony of Russell Oswald before the New York State Special Commission on Attica, April 28, 1972.

79.   Minutes of the Proceedings of a Budget Hearing on Correctional Services, held by the Senate Finance Committee and the Assembly Ways and Means Committee in the Assembly Parlor, The Capitol, Albany, New York, February 10, 1971, p. 6 (Mimeograph)

80.   Ibid.

81.   Ibid., p. 7.

82.   Testimony of Russell Oswald before the New York State Special Commission on Attica, April 28, 1972.

83.   Budget Hearings on Correctional Services before the Legislative Finance Committees, February 10, 1971, p. 8.

84.   Ibid., p. 22.

85.   Interview with Don Clifford, staff associate and author of the Greenberg Report, Senate Minority Finance Committee, February 28, 1975.

86.   A Review of Various Aspects of the New York State Correctional Program. A Report to the New York State Legislature by the Senate Finance Minority. Samuel Greenberg, Chairman. August 29, 1971 (hereinafter referred to as The Greenberg Report). (Mimeograph)

87.   Interview with Don Clifford, February 28, 1975.

88.   Press Release No. 71-012 from the office of Senator Samuel Greenberg, Chairman of the Senate Finance Minority, State Capitol, Albany, New York, August 29, 1971, p. 1.

89.   Ibid., p. 2

90.   Ibid.

91.   Interview with Don Clifford, February 28, 1975.

92. Ibid.

93. Ibid.

94. Interview with Russell G. Oswald, March 19, 1975.

95. Ibid.

96. The Official Report of the New York State Special Commission on Attica, p. 131.

97. Oswald, Attica, My Story, p. 17.

98. Interview with Russell G. Oswald, March 19, 1975.

99. For a discussion of the riot from the perspective of the inmates involved, See: Richard X. Clark The Brothers of Attica (New York Links Books, 1973)

100. Oswald, Attica My Story, p. 17.

101. Ibid., p. 13.

102. Ibid., p. 69.

103. Ibid., p. 79.

104. Ibid.

105. The Official Report of the New York State Special Commission on Attica p. 193. See also, "Self Esteem and Violence by Guards and State Troopers at Attica" by Ezra Stotland in Crouch, Editor, The Keepers, pp. 291-301.

106. Oswald, Attica, My Story, p. 88.

107. Ibid., p. 216.

108. Ibid.

109. The Official Report of the New York State Special Commission on Attica, p. 131.

110. Oswald, Attica, My Story, p. 118.

111. The Official Report of the New York State Special Commission on Attica, pp. 251-257.

112. Oswald, Attica, My Story, p. 102.

113. Ibid., p. 122.

114. Ibid., p. 237

115. The Official Report of the New York State Special Commission on Attica, p. 332.

116. Newsday, 23 September 1971, p. 4.

117. Ibid.

118. New York Times, 17 September 1971, p. 31.

119. Ibid.

120. Newsday, 21 January 1972.

121. Newsday, 9 May 1972.

122. Newsday, 21 January 1972.

123. Newsday, 23 September 1971, p. 4.

124. Newsday, 9 May 1972.

125. Ibid.

126. Newsday, 9 May 1972.

127. Buffalo Evening News, 3 March 1971.

128. Jon Margolis, Reporter for Newsday, in his article in Newsday, 23 September 1971, p.4.

129. Ibid.

130. Ibid.

131. Newsday, 21 Janaury 1972.

132. Sunday News, 19 September 1971.

133. Daily News, 20 September 1971.

134. Daily News, 18 September 1971, p.4.

135. Interview with Russell G. Oswald, March 19, 1975.

136. Interview with Senator John R. Dunne, March 17, 1975.

137. Interview with Vito Ternullo, May 9, 1974.

138. Newsday, 21 January 1972.

139. Ibid.

140. Minutes of a Budget Hearing held by the Senate Finance Committee and the Assembly Ways and Means Committee on the Budget of the Department of Correctional Services in the Assembly Parlor, The Capitol Building, Albany, New York, February 29, 1972, p.41.

141. Unfortunately the data cited in this section cannot be placed in a Table, for all of this data on budget cuts was obtained at "closed-door" legislative budget hearings and concerned the "proposed" Correctional Services Department budget; information not made public, since subject to review by the budget staff of the Division of the Budget and the Governor before being eventually incorporated into the Governor's Executive Budget (see Chapter two). Since the information was gleaned from a question and answer exchange between the legislative leaders and the correctional administration, it is difficult to classify by way of Tables.

142. See Footnote 140.

143. Ibid.

144. Ibid., p. 39.

145. Ibid., p.6.

146. Ibid., p.12.

147. Budget Hearing on Correctional Services before the Legislative Finance Committees, February 10, 1971, p.48.

148. Budget Hearing on Correctional Services before the Legislative Finance Committees, February 29, 1972, p.88.

149. Ibid.

150. Ibid., p. 91.

151. Ibid., p. 90.

152. Interview with Russell G. Oswald, March 19, 1975.

153. Ibid.

154. Ibid.

155. New York Times, 30 March 1972, p. 27.

156. The Official Report of the New York State Special Commission on Attica, pp. xvi-xix.

157. New York Times, 13 September 1972, p. 34.

158. Newsday, 24 May 1972.

159. New York State Legislative Program for 1973 by the Committee on Public Affairs, Community Service Society, New York, January 1973, pp. 12-13.

160. Ibid., pp. 13-15.

161. Alliance for a Safer New York Memorandum on New York State Legislative Proposals #72-650-108, pp. 1-8. (Mimeograph)

162. Robert H. Connery and Gerald Benjamin, Rockefeller of New York (Ithaca: Cornell University Press, 1979) p. 186.

163. New York Urban Coalition Legislative Memo, New York Urban Coalition, July 18, 1973, p. 1.

164. New York Times, 30 May 1973, p. 22.

165. New York Urban Coalition Legislative Memo, July 18, 1973, p. 1.

166. Ibid.

167. Interview with Senator John R. Dunne, March 17, 1975.

168. Barbara Lavin, Participant Observer, September 1967-September 1972.

169. New York Times, 12 June 1973, p. 26.

170. Ibid.

171. Ibid.

172. Ibid.

173. Ibid.

174. Interview with Russell G. Oswald, March 19, 1975.

175. Connery and Benjamin, <u>Rockefeller</u> <u>of</u> <u>New</u> <u>York</u>, p. 187.

CHAPTER V

THEORETICAL CONSIDERATIONS, ANALYSIS, AND CONCLUSIONS

The dearth of concern for the development of criminal justice theory has been noted in recent journal articles, (1) and a plea has been made to take into consideration the theoretical perspectives of other disciplines in order to elevate the field of criminal justice "to a more scientifically sophisticated level" beyond a mere description of facts. (2)

What then does this study have to offer by way of theoretical development? Since we have been presenting the historical data of the politics of prison reform during a particular period, we must ask ourselves in what way does this data contribute to a more general understanding of our world; in what way does it contribute towards an evaluation of the more general explanations (or theories) by which political scientists explain our political reality?

Much of conventional American political theory assumes a pluralist, conflict-oriented political system receptive to the demands of various interest groups holding relatively stable positions on public policy. This pluralist perspective thus assumes an open and fluid political system in which various interests, not necessarily the most powerful or influential, can at some point make their views known and hence influence the political decision making process. (3)

Foremost, pluralism assumes dispersal of power, (4) that is, that within the American political system there is no elite group in control of the decision making process. It assumes that all significant interests are represented in the political system and that the political leadership will respond to their demands. (5) The pluralist conception of the American political system evolved from and was in turn supportive of the American ideology and its concern with democracy, representative government, protection of individual rights and access to power. If the system can be shown to ignore certain interests, then the claim to the ideal of democracy would be threatened. But if the system is democratic, all of the interest groups noted in our study, namely the correctional bureaucracy, business/labor interests, religious/social reformers, and prison inmates should have been able to elicit some governmental responses to their demands.

Many of the pluralists are also conflict theorists, such as E.E. Schattschneider. For these pluralists, conflict among

121

competing interest groups widens the political arena to include less cohesive, less organized interests who can then appeal to the public authority for redress by publicizing and socializing the conflict.(6) As Schattschneider has noted, powerful special interests prefer private settlements because as the decision making process is socialized, the scope of conflict and consequently the balance of forces and the outcome change.(7) He thus implies that in any democratic system, the powerless will be heard only in an arena opened to a wider public through publicized conflict.

But what tends not to be examined by many pluralists is the nature of governmental response to the various interest groups. In his work on federal regulatory policy,(8) Murray Edelman examines this issue and classifies governmental response as falling into one or the other of two distinct categories - symbolic responses and tangible responses. Symbolic responses give the appearance of actual involvement and concern but without any direct resource allocation. These responses do not confer substantive material resources nor the power to decide their future allocation. Typical of symbolic responses would be: the inauguration of study commissions, appointment of task forces, press conferences, "the ribbon cutting, street corner ceremony. . . and the rhetorical flourishes with which 'massive attacks', 'comprehensive programs', and 'coordinated planning' are frequently promoted."(9) Tangible responses, on the other hand, consist in the retention or gain of substantial material resources such as money or property, or of political power to influence future political decisions regarding the allocation of money or property.

For Edelman, symbolic responses are used to quiet the masses without threatening the stability of the system nor the position of those with real influence within that system.

> The most obvious kinds of dissemination of symbolic satisfactions are to be found in administrative dicta accompanying decisions and orders, in press releases and in annual reports. It is not uncommon to give the rhetoric to one side and the decision to the other. . . . The integral connection is apparent between symbolic satisfaction of the disorganized on the one hand, and the success of the organized, on the other, in using governmental instrumentalities as aids in securing the tangible resources they claim.(10)

For Edelman, public officials may be said to respond tangibly to those constituent groups which are characterized by cohesiveness, continuity and a significant amount of resources and influence; on the other hand, public officials are likely to respond symbolically to those "powerless" protest groups or interests which do not have the political resources necessary to enter the bargaining arena.(11)

Abraham Blumberg, in his work, Criminal Justice also alludes to this distinction between form (rhetoric) and substance, between the symbolic and the tangible.

> Central to the notion of law and order is the promise that it will provide the machinery for orderly change in the allocation of rewards, opportunity structures and access to the means of life in our social system - in a word, justice. But in fact, our law enforcement, public welfare, mental hospital and court systems have become the very agencies which blunt the possibilities for orderly change and the more equitable allocation of life chances. Creditors, landlords, corporations, the wealthy and political machines tend to receive more favorable treatment from courts, legislatures and regulatory agencies, while consumers, debtors, wage-earners, the very young, the mentally ill, the deviant and the poor are short-changed. The former groups tend to receive the substance, the latter groups, the form of justice.(12)

And again one sees the proposition that government and system respond tangibly to those with resources, i.e., the creditors, landlords, wealthy, political machines and symbolically to those without political power, the consumers, debtors, wage-earners, deviants. Blumberg's statement coincides with the symbolic/tangible thesis even though he did not develop it in these terms.

Michael Lipsky has adequately stated the importance of research designed to analyze critically the pluralist conception of the American political system.(13) Any political system which proclaims itself open and responsive to group interests while consistently dispensing tangible material benefits to one group, and merely symbolic assurances to another, places in doubt the pluralist conception of that system.

123

Which then of these theoretical perspectives would seem to be supported by the data assembled in this study? What was the relative political effectiveness of the various interest groups present in the correctional arena and what was the nature of governmental response? A brief summary of the data and what it says about the relative explanatory power of the various theories is in order.

Conclusions and Theoretical Analysis

During the nineteenth and early twentieth centuries, business interests and those of the correctional administration were in harmony, because each had resources the other needed. Prisons needed sources of revenue and business was willing to supply that revenue in return for the cheap labor of the prison inmates which enabled business interests to profitably enter the incipient manufacturing market. The inroads made by business interests in this arena demonstrate the workings of the pluralist theoretical framework, that is, the system was open to the involvement of various interests.

However, as the free labor market outside the prison expanded, labor interests began to exert political pressure on the state legislature to restrict the use of prison labor and thereby eliminate their competitors; and labor interests were successful in having their demands met. The same theoretical perspective that explained business involvement in the system likewise explains labor involvement. And henceforth, prison-made goods were required by law to be marked "made in prison" in an effort to deter buyers. Later, manufacturing interests within prisons were restricted to the production of goods normally imported into the country from abroad; and finally only such goods as could be used and bought by state institutions could be produced within prison walls.

According to pluralist theory, business/labor interests were able to enter the correctional bargaining arena because they were organized, had political resources and hence were able to exert influence on the decision making process affecting that arena, thereby illustrating the openness and fluidity of the political system with no one permanent interest solely receiving benefits from the system.

The most prevailing interest within the correctional arena throughout the scope of this study was the correctional bureaucracy. Their influence and power resulted, in Schattschneider's terms, from a strictly privatized arena. They were able to receive substantive benefits from the system because no other interest was making conflicting demands for the available

124

resources.

From 1959 until the mid 1960s, in general, the judicial, executive and legislative branches of state government did not interfere in the workings of the prison system. The press and the public were virtually excluded from any contact with inmates. Administrative dicta restricting public access by way of censorship of correspondence, publications, and prison visits with inmates were upheld in the courts. Correctional administrators were given virtual autonomy in dealing with prison matters. And when the bureaucracy was able to deal in this privatized arena, they received tangible, substantive rewards from the system. This is illustrated by the analysis of the budgetary process and consideration of legislative proposals by the state legislature as presented in Chapter two.

In the late 1960s the correctional arena was widened to include other interests, and this widening of the arena was to modify the benefits the bureaucracy had been able to obtain previously. Increasing pressure for social change by civil liberties groups, urban violence, rising rates of crime and drug addiction and demands for stricter law enforcement widened the arena through conflict to include interests not previously involved in the correctional arena. The balance of forces was changing. In the socialization of the conflict and the widened arena that resulted, these other interests should have been heard, according to the pluralist perspective of Schattschneider. And this should have severely limited the influence of the bureaucracy in the correctional arena.

But the bureaucracy did not totally lose the previous power it possessed. Our analysis of the interests which surfaced in the socialization of this conflict during the mid 1960s indicates that the demands of some of these interests were indirectly beneficial to the correctional bureaucracy. Thus, the law enforcement interests, who demanded more severe prison sentences for criminal offenders as a crime deterrent and institutional "treatment" of narcotic addicts, achieved policies which in essence assisted the correctional bureaucracy. When a declining state prison population that resulted from federal court decisions affecting the criminally insane would have resulted in the loss of jobs, security, and hence of power, for the correctional bureaucracy, NACC was instituted and used existing bureaucratic correctional structures - vacant state prison facilities - as narcotic treatment facilities and correctional officers as narcotic treatment staff. Prisons thereby remained at capacity and correctional officers retained their job security. Likewise, demands by these same law enforcement interests for increased police protection, arrests, and convictions also increased prison clientele.

But as Chapter three indicates, study commissions such as the Governor's Special Committee on Criminal Offenders further enlarged the scope of conflict to include interests not in harmony with correctional bureaucratic interests. And this widening of the arena which permitted other interests to enter the decision - making process signaled a general loss of influence for the correctional bureaucracy, thereby supporting again pluralist conceptions of an open and fluid political system.

The correctional bureaucracy suffered an immediate loss of influence in their inability to prevent the unification of the Departments of Correction and Parole into a new Department of Correctional Services, a modified recommendation of the Governor's Special Committee on Criminal Offenders. The bureaucracy suffered a further loss of influence in their inability to prevent the Governor from nominating, or the Legislature from ratifying, the appointment of the former head of Parole, Russell G. Oswald, as the Commissioner of the new Department of Correctional Services.

The further widening of the arena in the 1970s had even more severe consequences for the bureaucracy. As Chapter four demonstrates, increasing pressure for social change by civil liberties groups and a receptivity by the federal courts made the prisons the target of public scrutiny especially in the judicial arena. Various court decisions, especially the Sostre decisions in the New York State jurisdiction, legally restricted the formerly autonomous position of correctional administrators, and the courts became the battleground for prisoner rights issues versus bureaucratic interests. The correctional bureaucracy did not win many of the federal court decisions that challenged their autonomy.

Prison inmates, essentially the powerless in any conflict, served to gain from a widening of the arena. For in Schattschneider's terms, only through a widened arena could their demands expect to be considered in the decision making process and evidence of their involvement would serve again to justify pluralist conceptions of the American political system.

This analysis indicates that prison inmates did benefit from this widening of the arena. The federal courts, which were responsive to prisoner demands as articulated by civil liberties groups, granted by law greater accessibility to reading materials, the press, legal aid and legislative and executive representatives by restricting the censorship formerly imposed by prison administrators. Federal court decisions such as those involving New York State prisoner, Martin Sostre, even ruled on permissible punishments to recalcitrant inmates. Work release provided for greater contact with the outside community and

126

enhanced an inmate's possibilities of viable employment upon release from the prison institution. Active recruitment of Black and Spanish-speaking correctional officers was initiated. Unsanitary penal living conditions were publicized in the media and, at times, issues such as lengthy pre-trial delays, disparity of sentencing, and disproportionate jailing of minorities also received public attention both in the press and on television. Also, rehabilitative positions increased 100% in male maximum security prisons; from 3% of the total prison staff in 1959 to 6.5% in 1973. Thus, prison inmates might also be said to have received tangible benefits from the system because of their involvement in the widened arena which included the federal courts and civil liberties groups willing to represent their interests.

The involvement of the religious/social reformers in the correctional arena must be considered separately. For while it is evident that many of their interests and demands coincided with inmate demands, however they never formed an alliance with these groups and never took an active, visible role in the street demonstrations that followed the riots at Auburn and Attica state prisons. This lack of activist involvement by the reformers is difficult to explain, although it is empirically verifiable.

Reformers became involved in the correctional arena at the time of the social welfare era (1800s), when the arena was populated not with professionals but with the wealthy. The reform involvement of this group was a reaction against the increasing numbers of immigrants, industrial workers and urban poor who did not share an upper class commitment to thriftiness, sobriety and the Protestant Work Ethic. The aim of these social reformers, according to some observers, was to convert the urban industrial poor to a middle class system of values, thus preserving the status quo.(14) Reformers may thus be seen as having limited goals which were generally non-controversial in the reform modality since the goals were not directed at broad system change but merely at socializing the poor, the deviant, the criminal into what the reformers viewed as the American way. In the area of corrections, there was wide agreement among reform groups such as NCCD, CSS, and CANY that inmates should have greater educational programs and more opportunity for job training and recreational programs. Family visiting, furloughs, work release, sanitary penal conditions, all were general reforms espoused in study commission reports dating back to 1915 and, as such, among reformers, were not controversial.

Moreover, the reformers did not come under fire from other segments in the arena such as law enforcement or bureaucratic interests which might have opposed their reform goals. Indeed the fact that the reformers did not become the object of controversy within the arena indicates their conservative stance. And according to Banfield, this avoidance of controversy was important in order to maintain their own association.(15)

The widening of the arena then served to publicize reform goals specified earlier in study commission reports, but the limited goals of these religious/social reformers, their non-controversial stance and concern for self-maintenance generally made them an ineffective force for change.

Thus the widened arena of Schattschneider would seem to validate pluralist theory for it demonstrates that as the conflict was socialized other interests entered the arena and affected the decision making process. All groups seem to have been accorded benefits from the system, but the amount and nature of the benefits received were disparate. And this issue of the nature of benefits accorded interests in the system is never even raised by the pluralists. Thus we turn to Edelman for a clearer analysis of how the widened arena affected the benefits accorded the various interests.

An analysis of the aftermath of the prison riots at Attica and Auburn indicates that not only did the bureaucracy not suffer a permanent loss of influence, but they actually received substantive benefits from the system. Correctional bureaucratic demands for increased spending for locking devices, riot control equipment, additional correction officers, and the institution of a "maxi-maxi" at each maximum security prison were met. The widened arena, then, did not provide for a permanent shift of decisions or resources to other groups; the bureaucracy was able to sustain its power and influence even after the violence of the prison riots.

The inmates received some benefits which primarily served to ameliorate their condition within the prison. Inmates did receive access to the courts but court intervention in prison policy is of such an ambiguous nature that this will be discussed more completely in the final chapter. Suffice it to say now that the benefits accorded inmates did not substantively change their status and did not insure for them a future role in the decision - making process. Even the 100% increase in "rehabilitative" staff positions in the male maximum security prisons should not be considered substantive since rehabilitative staff positions still totalled only 6.5% of the total prison staff and, in many cases, these positions were filled with existing bureaucratic personnel as both Commissioners Oswald and McGinnis have testified.(16) The benefits thus accorded prison inmates did not significantly alter their power position vis-a-vis the correctional bureaucracy. The correctional bureaucracy, by 1973, remained in firm control of the prison institutions. The problem remains as to how to classify even the token benefits accorded the inmates.

Edelman's framework provides for only a clear-cut distinction between symbolic and tangible response. And certainly throughout this work, there are instances of a purely symbolic response, especially in the appointment of the "post-riot" study commissions of 1915, 1931, and 1973.(17) The role of the reform groups, such as the State Council of NCCD called together "once" in an advisory capacity to the Governor's Special Committee on Criminal Offenders, can also be considered a symbolic response to reform interests. However, the problem remains as to how to analyze and compare governmental response where disparate tangible benefits were accorded the opposing interests of the bureaucracy and the prison inmates. And one of the problems in utilizing Edelman's mode of analysis is that he fails to define or elucidate "quantity" or "quality" of tangible responses.(18)

Edelman's definitions of symbolic/tangible rewards are mutually exclusive, as mentioned earlier. A tangible response is one which allocates material benefits. A symbolic response does not allocate material benefits but satisfies demands merely in the perception (minds) of the people involved. While such a distinction enables one to critically examine the use of such responses as the appointment of study commissions, such as the McKay Commission, without the allocation of resources to implement their recommendations, and has the advantage of being discrete, that is, "symbolic" or "tangible", it nevertheless is not without its shortcomings. The thrust of Edelman's critical analysis could be frustrated by the allocation of manifestly inadequate resources - even one penny - by the government to the resolution of any particular demand. Hence any amount of money given by the government to the poor might be considered an example of tangible response to the "War on Poverty". The critical thrust of Edelman's analysis thus demands a further distinction between "token" tangible and "substantive" tangible. But this distinction by its very nature would not be so clear-cut or operationally definable. While symbolic/tangible are clear-cut and mutually exclusive definitions, the terms, "token" and "substantive" both refer to tangible responses and, while these terms are nominally distinct, they suffer from the defects of any merely nominal definition for purposes of empirical analysis, that is, they do not sufficiently specify concrete phenomena. A "token" response might nominally be defined as the allocation of insufficient resources to meet the demand in the objective world, but like Edelman's symbolic response, would merely assure people mentally that the problem is being solved. A "substantive" tangible response might be the allocation of sufficient resources to meet the demand of the interests involved and sufficiency might be judged from the common sense opinions of informed critics.

129

However, it is the theorist's responsibility and choice as to how one is to operationalize these nominal definitions. Thus one might operationally define "token" as less than a specified percentage of the total funding required to meet total demand. However, these operational definitions must also meet the complex requirements for applicability and validity. Whatever the problems involved in the operational definition of "substantive" tangible and "token" tangible, we should not let this obscure their analytical utility. As C. Wright Mills has warned, sometimes publicly relevant issues may be obscured by meeting methodological requirements.(19)

It is interesting to note that these questions were never raised by the critics of Edelman's book, The Symbolic Uses of Politics. In classifying Edelman in the symbolic - psychological mode, these readers failed to consider either the political impact or the methodological problems inherent in Edelman's work.(20)

Ultimately, Edelman asserts that symbols serve to tranquilize group interest.

> Only through symbolic reassurances that "the state" recognizes the claims and status of the group as legitimate is quiescence brought about and the reassurance must be periodically renewed. It is through speeches, gestures, and settings that evoke reassuring anticipations that men's political claims are limited and the public order maintained.(21)

The issues thus raised by Edelman are critical to an understanding of the true nature of political, governmental or system responsiveness. As the present study indicates, the responsiveness of the system to such powerless groups as prison inmates is most often in the nature of a symbolic or token tangible response. This finding therefore serves to further restrict pluralist conceptions of system responsiveness to interest group activity. Edelman's perspective must be considered together with our suggested refinements of it if we wish to discover more about the nature of stability and change within the political system.

In sum, our data would tend to restrict, if not refute, the more optimistic claims of political scientists of the pluralistic persuasion. In general, those with established political power received tangible allocation of resources while those without such power (prison inmates) received merely symbolic or token responses.

One additional criticism of the pluralistic perspective might also be noted, namely, the disparities of effort or types of mechanisms through which the various groups managed to receive the responses from government. Those with established political power frequently managed to achieve tangible responses through established administrative channels (for example, the budgetary process, personal contacts, organized union power). Those without such established political power tended to be ignored by government until they managed to attract attention temporarily through more drastic efforts such as prison riots or public demonstrations. Clearly then, disparate efforts are needed by different groups if a pluralistic governmental response is to be achieved. Here again Edelman's analysis is useful: even when outsider groups have succeeded in making their voices heard, the real issue tends to be defused by symbolic or token responses such as study commissions or the allocation of manifestly inadequate resources.

This type of analysis is important to the field of criminal justice because the decisions affecting criminal justice take place in the broader political arena.

Endnotes-Chapter V

1.   Frank Williams, "The Demise of the Criminological Imagination: A Critique of Recent Criminology" in Justice Quarterly 1:1, March 1984, pp. 91-106.
     See also: Cecil L. Willis, Criminal Justice Theory: A Case of Trained Incapacity" in Journal of Criminal Justice 11:5 (1983) pp. 447-458.

2.   Willis, "Criminal Justice Theory: A Case of Trained Incapacity," p. 454.

3.   The pluralist perspective is readily found in the works of the following authors: Sandor Halebsky, Mass Society and Political Conflict (Cambridge: Cambridge University Press, 1976), p. 282. See also footnotes 8, 9, 10; David Truman, The Governmental Process (New York: Knopf Publishing Company, 1951); Charles Lindblom, The Intelligence of Democracy (New York: Macmillan Press, 1965)
     Robert Dahl, Preface to Democratic Theory (Chicago: University of Chicago Press, 1956) Nelson Polsby, Community Power and Political Theory (New Haven: Yale University Press, 1963); E.E. Schattschneider, The Semi-Sovereign People (New York Holt, Rinehart and Winston, 1960).

4.   Halebsky, Mass Society and Political Conflict, p. 188.

5.   Ibid.

6.   Schattschneider, The Semi-Sovereign People, p. 40.

7.   Ibid., See also: Theodore Lowi, "American Business, Public Policy, Case Studies and Political Theory", World Politics 16:4 (July 1964) Published by Princeton University Press.

8.   Murray Edelman, The Symbolic Uses of Politics (Chicago: University of Illinois Press, 1967)

9.   Michael Lipsky, Protest in City Politics (Chicago: Rand McNally & Company, 1970) p. 176.

10. Edelman, The Symbolic Uses of Politics, p. 39.

11. Lipsky, Protest in City Politics, Chapter 7
     Edelman, The Symbolic Uses of Politics, Chapter 2.

12. Abraham Blumberg, Criminal Justice Second Edition (New York: New Viewpoints (Franklin Watts), 1979) pp. 358-359.

13.   Lipsky, Protest in City Politics, p. 200.

14.   Anthony Platt, The Child Savers, (Chicago, University of Chicago Press, 1969)
      See also: Joseph Gusfield, Symbolic Crusade (Chicago: University of Illinois Press, 1963) for an analysis of the religious/social reform involvement in the American Temperance Movement, especially pp. 79-80; Edward C. Banfield, Political Influence (New York: The Free Press, 1961) pp. 297-299; Edward C. Banfield, The Unheavenly City Revisited (Boston: Little, Brown and Co., 1974) for a more recent analysis of the malaise of the lower classes as "present" rather than "future" oriented; and Herbert Gans, "The Positive Functions of Poverty", American Journal of Sociology, 78:2 (September 1972) p. 280.

15.   Banfield, Political Influence, p. 297.

16.   See Chapter four of this work.

17.   Anthony Platt, in his book, The Politics of Riot Commissions (New York: Collier Books, 1971) denotes the symbolic effect of riot commissions by an analysis of the composition, ideology, and mandate of eight major riot commissions in America from 1917-1970.   See especially, Introduction pp. 3-54.

18.   Edelman, Symbolic Uses of Politics, p. 42.

19.   C. Wright Mills, The Sociological Imagination (New York: Oxford University Press, 1959) pp. 50-55.

20.   The following book reviews of The Symbolic Uses of Politics: Bennis, in The Annals of the American Academy (September 1965) London Times Literary Supplement, 22 April 1965, p. 309; James C. Davis in American Political Science Review 59:3 (September 1965) pp. 695-696.   Harold Lasswell in American Journal of Sociology 70:6 (May 1965) p. 735.   Nor are these methodological issues raised by researchers noting the symbolic/tangible framework - such as Myron Puckett's study of "Successful Protest Movements in School Districts", Urban Education (April 1976).

21.   Edelman, Symbolic Uses of Politics, p. 193.   For a further development of Edelman's work and an excellent general discussion of symbols in politics, see also: Charles Elder and Roger Cobb, The Political Uses of Symbols (New York: Longman, Inc., 1983).

CHAPTER VI

AFTERWORD: 1974-1984

This study has been primarily concerned with correctional policy making during the Governorship of Nelson A. Rockefeller. We saw that at the end of his administration the gains that had been made by the inmates in the courts were being threatened by the retributive reaction to the riots at Auburn and especially at Attica. After the riots, the prison guards seemed to be benefitting directly from increased expenditures for security personnel and better locking devices. The Legislature seemed to be more responsive to the demands of the guards and apparently much less so to inmate demands.

An update is warranted in order to assess the relative balance of power between these two most enduring political interests in the New York State correctional arena and this discussion will take us into 1984.

The Commissioner currently at the helm of the state's Department of Correctional Services (DOCS) is Thomas Coughlin, a former New York State Trooper and Retired Staff Sergeant - U.S. Air Force, and former Deputy Commissioner for Mental Retardation in the state Department of Mental Hygiene. Although his work in mental health might indicate a general rehabilitative stance, this would be a misreading. Coughlin's academic training is in Public Administration, not social work, and there is evidence that he was chosen because of his law enforcement background. The head of the search committee which recommended Coughlin to then Governor Hugh Carey in 1979 has noted the reasons for his appointment. "He was a cop. He had run a large state agency and clearly he had compassion."[1]

And Coughlin clearly has not abandoned his law enforcement background. In 1979, he was appointed Commissioner with intent "to bring order to the system."[2] In 1982, Coughlin was chosen as the Governor's liaison with local law enforcement and public protection agencies. In this regard, Coughlin follows in the footsteps of his immediate predecessor, Benjamin Ward, a former Deputy Commissioner of Police and Traffic Commissioner before being named Corrections Commissioner. In 1984, Ward was appointed New York City Commissioner of Police, the final step in a career which had begun in 1951 as patrolman. Historically, Commissioners of State Corrections in New York have come from the field of law enforcement, as did Paul McGinnis, a former New York State Trooper with whom we began this study. In this history, Russell Oswald, social worker, remains an anomaly.

That Commissioner Coughlin identifies with the law enforcement interests might best be illustrated by his relationship with the correctional officers. You may recall from the previous chapter that Russell Oswald never did win their support or acceptance.

One of Coughlin's first tasks was indeed to restore order to a system crippled by a sixteen day strike by the unionized correction officers. As the Commissioner has stated,

> the correction officers had received no real benefits from the Attica riot and they felt they were being ignored. I decided to bring some balance into the system by responding to the group I would consider my constituency - the correction officers and especially the union, because they were an organized, cohesive group - an enduring force.(3)

Thus, the Commissioner held town meetings at each prison institution and made the central office visible by bringing with him all of the Deputy Commissioners. It was a mix of formality and informality since after the union-sponsored meetings, beer was served to all who were present. Coughlin has noted that, like the town meetings, some of the benefits conferred on the officers were minor in fact, but important to them. "The correction officers were unhappy about the new uniforms (a collegiate type blazer and slacks) and wanted to return to the old. I granted their request, gave them a tie, hat, belt and new arm patch."(4)

That Coughlin was able to win the support of the correction officers then and has been able to sustain it for the past several years is perhaps best illustrated by a statement made during the Ossining Prison riot in 1983 by John Burke, Executive Director of the council representing the correction officers. Burke stated, "in twenty five years. . . he's the best I've ever seen. I thank God that some of the Commissioners in the past were not in charge."(5)

Thomas Coughlin is also reputed to "have the respect of at least some inmates" because he is willing to sit down with inmate committees, solicits letters from them and "reads them".(6) And in the wake of the problems associated with severe overcrowding, Coughlin has not had to deal publicly with any other prison riot in the two years since the Ossining prison riot in January of 1983.(7)

Nevertheless, the system remains riddled with tensions which have resulted in increased confrontations and assaults within the facilities. Some observers express surprise that these tensions have not resulted in additional prison riots. And Coughlin has noted that "things are much more tenuous now."(8)

Many of the problems and tensions within the New York State system are also issues of concern to prison administrators throughout the United States. Overcrowded penal facilities is perhaps the problem of concern to most administrators in the 1980s. In 1970, 356,000 persons were confined in prisons and jails throughout the entire United States, but in 1977, this number had increased to approximately 530,000 and was "growing at a rate of about 1,000 a week."(9) In New York State, there was a 100% increase in the prison population from 1972 to 1983.(10) Ten thousand additional inmates flooded the system between January 1979 and November 1983.(11)

This notable increase in prisoners apparently caught the Department of Correctional Services (DOCS) by surprise. The Department's estimated population for fiscal year 1982 was too low by 4,000 inmates.(12) In the rush to provide additional space, annexes and modular units were hastily constructed. Sections of state mental institutions and "space not previously designated as housing" in existing facilities (i.e. program and support services space) were converted into housing for inmates.(13)

The budget of the New York State Department of Correctional Services thus increased 80% in four years, from $424 million in 1979 to $764 million in 1983 - a direct result of capital construction projects. By way of comparison, in 1959, the budget was $40 million. In 1959, there were five maximum security institutions, one medium security prison and a sprinkling of work camps near the Canadian border. In 1984, there were thirteen maximum security facilities, twenty-two medium security and sixteen minimum security facilities.(14) Thousands of new prison cells have been added and still the demand increases. In 1959, there were approximately 10,000 prisoners in state correctional facilities; in 1984, there were approximately 33,000.(15)

One might wonder about the status of rehabilitative programming in light of the massive funds expended for capital construction and in light of the overcrowded conditions that persist despite the continuing creation of new cells.

At least one reform group, the Correctional Association of New York, mentioned earlier in this study, has reported that conditions at Attica in 1982 were worse than before the riot in 1971. The report entitled Attica 1982 cited overcrowded conditions, inadequate medical care, deficiencies in food services, reduction in recreation time, inadequate availability of job training

137

or counseling programs, inadequacy of legal materials and restricted use of the law library. The report also stated that

> whereas five years ago, a prisoner in an academic program would attend school for five hours per day, today (1982) a prisoner in an 'academic education' program generally spends only one 45-60 minute period during the day in class.(16)

These reformers also contended that the reduction in available programming had resulted in an increased number of "idle" prisoners who had to be locked in their cells for some twenty-two hours a day.(17) Furthermore, they stated that system-wide the number of "idle" prisoners doubled between January 1981 and December 1981 and that at Attica, twenty-five percent of the inmates were so confined.(18)

Commissioner Coughlin has called into question the accuracy of this reform document, noting that "Attica is not worse today than before the riot. . . . Inmates are out of their cells from 7 AM to 11 PM."(19) The Commissioner has also questioned the basis on which an inmate might be considered "idle".

> If the inmate is in an education program for 2-3 hours per day and spends the rest of the time in recreation, should he be counted idle?. . . . Some of the inmates, who have not been in school for ten years, cannot spend much more than 2-3 hours a day in such a program.(20)

But in the 1982-83 Budget it was noted that "an unanticipated increase in the inmate population and the resulting shortage of housing space has had a corollary impact on DOCS' ability to provide adequate programming for inmates during the past year."(21) And in the 1984-85 Budget, it was noted that funds were needed "to increase programming opportunities for the growing number of unemployed inmates."(22) In fact, the Commissioner has noted that the correctional industry program at Attica has been expanded to include a new midnight to 8 AM shift in order to accommodate idle prisoners.(23) Clearly it would seem that job training and educational programs are not at the level espoused by earlier reform groups.

And the classification system proposed by reformers to individualize "treatment" of offenders with regard to education or job training is being used instead to identify and segregate the violent offenders from the rest of the inmate population. Under a federal grant in the early 1980s, the Department of Correctional Services developed a system to measure and document "inmate risk to the institution and community" in order to provide "specialized treatment in a segregated setting." It was noted that this program "not only permits the early identification and treatment of the needs of problem inmates but enhances the Department's ability to manage the general inmate population."(24) (Emphasis mine)

Among the concerns of the correction officers in New York in the 1980s, would be listed, the increasing incidence of AIDS among state inmates, the fact that the correction officers feel that the administration is favorably inclined to some inmate concerns while they (correction officers) are more concerned with security,(25) and the increasing number of inmates convicted of a violent felony offense (46.5% of new commitments in 1978, 63.6% of new commitments in 1982). (26)

The correction officers' union has likewise renewed its demands for additional "maxi-maxi" units (Involuntary Protection Unit) for troublesome inmates such as the one established at Great Meadow Prison.(27) At the Attica segregation unit, twenty new plexiglass cells with only small holes for ventilation have been installed.(28)

The severe overcrowding has resulted in a scene reminiscent of the marching manoeuvres of the old Auburn System of the nineteenth century. It has been noted that in 1982, at Attica Prison, prisoners must keep a rule of silence in the corridors and "are required to march two abreast to the commands of accompanying guards throughout the institution."(29) The Commissioner himself has noted that the "paramilitary" nature of the organization makes it an easier Department to run than Mental Retardation. "Here, when I give an order, they practically salute, at Mental Retardation, when I gave an order, the staff of psychologists and psychiatrists would say 'Let's talk about that'."(30)

Inmate Liaison Committees established in 1971 as a reform measure to serve as a conduit of information and complaints between the administration and inmates appear to have been subverted. These Committees instituted at each state prison in New York State were to be composed of elected representatives from the administrative staff, correction officers and inmates. The authors of Attica 1982 state that although the administration at Attica considers the ILC a viable body, inmate representatives refer to the Committee as "virtually defunct, given no authority over institutional matters, often little respect by the administration and generally ignored by all parties."(31)

Furthermore, the grievance mechanism established by Correction Law Section 139 to "fairly, simply and expeditiously handle inmate complaints" has become another source of frustration at Attica State Prison. Inmates complain of time delays, lack of meaningful resolution and restrictions on what issues can be brought before the committee. The committee cannot be used for concerns which have existing appeals mechanisms, "class action" issues affecting more than one prisoner, nor a grievance against any employee because of harassment or continuing abuse.(32) Officers are not required nor even requested to appear before the committee and no notation appears on the employee's record.(33)

Moreover there is a Catch-22 aspect to the grievance proceedings as far as inmates are concerned. Prisoners may not seek judicial relief in the courts until they have "exhausted" their administrative appeals, including the grievance process where relevant. (34) Inmate representatives on the Attica Grievance Committee noted that "we're thought of as nothing by the prisoners because of our lack of success in the grievance process."(35) Even the State Supreme Court has felt compelled to intervene in such administrative matters. In Hunyadi v. Smith (1982) the court found "that solely because of the allegation contained in a grievance filed by him, a prisoner became the subject of a disciplinary report for 'lying about an officer'."(36) Court action was required to have the disciplinary report expunged from the prisoner's record.(37)

It is interesting to note that perhaps the most enduring legacy from the late 1960s and 1970s is this involvement of the courts in prisoners' issues. Thus despite the more conservative law and order stance espoused by legislative and community interests, federal district courts continue to exert a liberal presence.

Many of the 1980 federal court decisions have focused on the issue of overcrowding in state prisons and local jails. For example, a Federal District judge in New Jersey used the strongest language in charging the city of Newark with "egregious and flagrant unconstitutional conditions" in the city's jails. Conditions were said to constitute "cruel and unusual punishment" and subject the inmates to "life threatening and health threatening conditions."(38) This decision echoes similar findings in the Washington State case of Hoptowit v. Ray.(39)

In New York State, the Department of Correctional Services was enjoined to accept within forty-eight hours of sentencing all state sentenced inmates on Rikers Island in New York City in order to ease overcrowding at that city facility.(40) And in November of 1983, Judge Morris Lasker of the Federal District

Court in Manhattan ordered New York City to comply with a limit he had placed on the number of pre-trial inmates in the House of Detention for Men on Rikers Island. This order resulted in the release of some 600 prisoners to the streets of New York.(41)

Continued involvement of the courts in the state correctional system prompted the Commissioner of Corrections to request additional funding in the 1982-83 fiscal year in order to reorganize and expand the Counsel's office, adding four new attorney positions and two part time legal assistants. The funding was needed "to respond to the large and growing volume of potentially precedent-setting inmate litigation."(42) The DOCS currently (1984) has twenty-three full time lawyers on its payroll.(43) In 1971, there were two lawyers on staff.

In New York State in recent years, courts have mandated medical staffing ratios and standards (Todaro v. Ward)(44) and improvements in food service "including the purchase of new equipment and the setting up of a Food Service Sanitation course for the prisoner-workers" (Ifill v. Smith(1981)(45) - matters previously handled internally by the correctional administration.

But at the same time, especially on a national level, there is evidence of a swing to the political right and a return to the "hands-off" court policies of an earlier time.

Evidence of this swing to the political right abounds. Executive proposals from the White House call for limitations on free legal assistance to indigent defendants, longer prison sentences and restrictions on Parole. New state laws in New York require mandatory prison sentences for drug abusers, violent criminals and repeat offenders. This has resulted in increased numbers of prisoners serving longer prison terms.(46) Indeed, in the move to determinate sentencing, some states have abolished their parole system. (In 1983, the New York State parole system came under fire when several parolees were re-arrested for felony offenses. In 1984, a proposal was put forth to unite Parole and Proabation in one agency to be called the New York State Division of Correctional Services, perhaps in an attempt to save parole jobs should public pressure continue for its demise).

In addition, there is now talk of inmate abuse of the right to court access and suggestions abound to limit inmate action in the filing of legal appeals. Victims are being invited to take part in court proceedings and in some instances, have been asked their opinion regarding a "just and equitable sentence". And in two recent Supreme Court decisions, the court held that Miranda rights need not always be read immediately if the public safety is threatened, and illegally seized evidence now may be introduced at a trial if "its eventual discovery through other, legal means was inevitable."(47)

As Stastny and Tyrnauer have noted,

> . . . after a period of massive judicial intervention, there now has begun a retreat. The Courts, in a time of increasingly conservative judicial appointments and in the wake of the conservative swing of public opinion have found ways of reinstating the "hands-off' policy in all but name. (48)

The Rhodes v. Chapman (1981) Supreme Court decision noted that the considerations used by the district court "properly are weighed by the legislative and prison administrators rather than a court."(49) According to Stastny and Tyrnauer, this was a "decidedly less inmate-oriented interpretation of the ban on cruel and unusual punishment."(50)

And yet the legacy of court involvement in the 1970s remains to some extent and forms a basis for inmate law suits in the 1980s. As Commissioner Thomas Coughlin has noted, many of the federal district court judges are Lyndon Johnson appointees and their liberal involvement continues and will continue for some time until the more conservative Supreme Court decisions filter down to the lower courts.(51)

Thus in 1981, an estimated ten to fifteen thousand inmates filed suits under Section 1983 of the Civil Rights Act as a consequence of a 1974 decision in Wright v. Toomey (74-1106-7th CA affirming Dist.Ct.) which upheld the right of inmates to sue for personal damages against prison officials.(52) Commissioner Coughlin has noted that he sees no lessening of court involvement in correctional matters in 1984.(53)

Federal involvement likewise continues in the area of funding. This too is a legacy from the 1970s. Thus the Correctional Services Department budget for 1981-82 noted receipt of federal funds from: the National Institute of Corrections; Title 1 and Title 4 money from the Department of Education (for supplementary remediation assistance and school lunch programs for state inmates); CETA funds (for training opportunities in clerical, medical, and fiscal support operations); Office of Vocational Rehabilitation and LEAA funds.

But as in the swing to the political right in public opinion and Supreme Court decisions, there is evidence of a future decline in federal funding for state corrections. "Elimination of

142

LEAA funding and the redirection of National Institute of Drug Abuse grants will force the reduction of drug treatment programs at (four facilities) unless the federal government restores the necessary funding."(54)

Nevertheless, federal funding was anticipated in the 1984-85 fiscal year for "AIDS research, rehabilitation of sex offenders and training facility staff in dealing with special populations."(55) And these funds from various federal agencies and national institutes were not to be insignificant, an expected $500,000.(56) And yet the emphasis is on "special problems", not on general job training or educational programs for the general population of inmates. Might this then be counted more as "control" rather than general rehabilitative programming?

Despite some new programs since the Attica riot, such as the Family Reunion Program which permits family or conjugal visits on the grounds of the prison, and continued increases in the inmate wage, the number of incidents of violence or self destruction continues to escalate. In 1981, 5,300 disciplinary proceedings were held; in the first ten months of 1983, over 7,000 were held and inmate grievances which totaled 7,200 in 1980 had escalated to 1,000 a month in 1983.(57)

Thus, despite continued court involvement and the federal funding of some programs, the correctional institutions in New York State remain riddled with tension and acts of violence. Neither the involvement of the courts nor the funded modifications seem to be sufficient tension relieving mechanisms in New York State. Besides as Stastny and Tyrnauer note,

> there is often a large gap between the rulings of the courts concerning prisoners rights and their implementation. . . courts in any event have a limited capacity to monitor administrative decision making and enforce standards within the prison. . . . The effective carrying out of a court's mandate necessarily assumes a substantial amount of good faith on the part of the prison administration and staff.(58)

It might also be suggested that access of prisoners to the courts merely rectifies wrongs already prohibited by law or accords already legal rights only on an individual basis, in a particular case. Thus such access alone does not insure sweeping policy change and may result merely in the amelioration of a "personal trouble" and not the resolution of a "public issue" to use the phraseology of C. Wright Mills.

143

Thus it seems clear that nearly fifteen years after the Attica riot, the correctional system seems destined to a return of the internally directed secure custodial administration facilitated by an "outsiders - hands-off" policy, which characterized the 1950s. As Commissioner Coughlin has noted, "my job is made easier by the absence of any political constituency."(59) That he is on his way to receiving almost a free hand in determining correctional policy in New York State is also confirmed by his statement that he has not found "any resistance on the part of the legislature or government to fund what we need. . . it's not a matter of money."(60)

Plus ça change, plus c'est la même chose.

1. Statement by Meyer S. Fruchter, New York State Deputy Director of Employee Relations, as quoted in the New York Times. January 11, 1983, p. B4.

2. Personal correspondence from Walter Chattman, Office of Community Relations (DOCS) November 30, 1983.

3. Interview with Commissioner Thomas Coughlin, Albany, New York, June 27, 1984.

4. Ibid.

5. As quoted in the New York Times, January 11, 1983, p.B4.

6. Ibid.

7. Demands made by rioting inmates at the Ossining Correctional Facility, thirty miles north of New York City, in January of 1983 were remarkably similar to the demands voiced by prison inmates in the 1970s. Major issues at Ossining concerned: overcrowded conditions, a lack of educational, vocational and recreational programs and restricted visitation and mail rights for the transient population awaiting placement in other prison facilities. (New York Times, January 10, 1983, p. B4).
   Although seventeen guards were held hostage for two days, the matter was resolved when the correctional administration, in conjunction with the Governor's Office, allowed the inmates' demands to be read on television news broadcasts. (New York Times, January 11, 1983, p. 1) Subsequently, the hostages were released by the inmates. Since no one was killed and the state did not have to resort to a forceful takeover, the matter soon disappeared from public notice.

8. Interview with Thomas Coughlin, June 27, 1984.

9. As quoted in Richard McGee, Prisons and Politics. (Lexington: D.C Heath and Co., 1981) p. 108.

10. New York Times, January 10, 1983, p. B4.

11. Personal correspondence from Walter Chattman, November 30, 1983.

12. New York State Executive Budget. Department of Correctional Services 1982-1983, p. 38.

13. Ibid., and the New York Times, January 12, 1983, p. B5.

14. New York State Executive Budget. Department of Correctional Services 1984-1985, p. 116.

15. Interview with Thomas Coughlin, June 27, 1984.

16. Attica 1982. Report by the Correctional Association of New York. Written by Don Pochoda, Consultant. Published in New York City, September 1982, p. 10.

17. Ibid., p. 9.

18. Ibid.

19. Interview with Thomas Coughlin, June 27, 1984.

20. Ibid.

21. New York State Executive Budget. Department of Correctional Services 1982-1983, p. 42.

22. New York State Executive Budget. Department of Correctional Services 1984-1985, p. 110.

23. Interview with Thomas Coughlin, June 27, 1984.

24. New York State Executive Budget. Department of Correctional Services 1981-1982, p. 99.

25. New York State Executive Budget. Department of Correctional Services, 1984-1985, p. 112, and interview with Henry Rosado, Correction Officer, Downstate Correctional Facility, Fishkill, New York, in Poughkeepsie, New York, April 1984.

26. New York State Executive Budget. Department of Correctional Services 1984-1985, p. 113.

27. Attica 1982, p. 23.

28. Ibid., p. 21.

29. Ibid., p. 7.

30. Interview with Thomas Coughlin, June 27, 1984.

31. Attica 1982, p. 15.

32. Ibid., pp. 15-16.

146

33. Ibid., p. 17.

34. Ibid.

35. Ibid., p. 16.

36. Ibid., p. 18.

37. Ibid.

38. New York Times, February 3, 1984, p. 1.

39. Charles Stastny and Gabrielle Tyrnauer, Who Rules the Joint? (Lexington: D.C. Heath and Co., 1982) p. 194.

40. New York State Executive Budget. Department of Correctional Services 1982-1983, p. 38.

41. New York Times, February 19, 1984, p. 56.

42. New York State Executive Budget. Department of Correctional Services 1982-1983, p. 38.

43. Interview with Thomas Coughlin, June 27, 1984.

44. Cited in the New York State Executive Budget. Department of Correctional Services, 1981-1982, p. 98.

45. Attica 1982, p. 12.

46. New York Times, January 10, 1983, p. B4.

47. New York v. Quarles 104 S. Ct 2626 (1984) re: Miranda rights and Nix v. Williams 104 S. Ct. 2501 (1984) re: illegally seized evidence. Also cited in Time magazine June 25, 1984, p. 63.

48. Stastny and Tyrnauer, Who Rules the Joint? p. 189.

49. Ibid., p. 198.

50. Ibid.

51. Interview with Thomas Coughlin, June 27, 1984.

52. Stastny and Tyrnauer, Who Rules the Joint? p. 189 and footnote #3, p. 199.

53. Interview with Thomas Coughlin, June 27, 1984.

54.   New   York   State   Executive   Budget.   Department   of
Correctional Services, 1981-1982, p. 98.

55.   New   York   State   Executive   Budget.   Department   of
Correctional Services, 1984-1985, p. 111.

56.   Ibid.

57.   Ibid., p. 113.

58.   Stastny and Tyrnauer, Who Rules the Joint?, pp. 189-190.

59.   Interview with Thomas Coughlin, June 27, 1984.

60.   Testimony   given   in   Benjamin   v.   Malcolm   (SDNY)   July   28,
1981) as quoted in Attica 1982, p. 26.

Author's Methodological Note

This work utilized the case study approach to the analysis of the politics of decision making in the area of correctional policy, specifically in New York State. However, on a more general level, it was intended as a concrete test of various political science theoretical approaches to the understanding of political decision making, specifically of the limitations of the pluralist approaches of authors such as Dahl and Schattschneider and of the utility of the more critical approach of authors such as Murray Edelman.

A variety of supplementary research techniques were used, the principal one being that of participant-observer. In addition, central participants were interviewed for the clarification and verification of otherwise unavailable information and a review of relevant publications and official documents was conducted for further verification of data in matters uncovered as the study progressed. Where such supplementary verification was not available, the author has footnoted the fact that the observations were based on her observations alone.

Since the author was working in the New York State correctional arena as: Research Assistant to the Chairman of the Senate Committee on Crime and Corrections, John R. Dunne; Special Assistant to the Director of the Women's Unit, Governor's Office during Nelson A. Rockefeller's administration; Assistant Director of the Alliance for a Safer New York and Board Member of the Women's Prison Association, a general familiarity with issues, actors and events was reasonably available. Although the author's status throughout the study was that of participant-observer, one of the most basic problems to this methodology, namely the difficulty of observer caused events (Hawthorne effect), did not occur since the decision - making occurred on a much higher administrative level and was not dependent on any active involvement by this observer.

The author, moreover, consciously strove to be as neutral as possible in the observation and recording of data, verifying her observations where possible through the supplementary research techniques noted above.

While one case study is not conclusive evidence about the utility of a general theoretical approach, nevertheless, it is one of the body of cases which might validate that approach. When a reasonable sampling of cases supports or fails to support a theory then that theory must be accepted, modified or rejected in accordance with the evidence.

149

However, one case study also may bring to light hitherto ignored influences or variables which may aid other researchers in their studies. Hopefully, this particular case study has illuminated some previously unexamined areas in the politics of correctional decision- making.

TABLE 1

BREAKDOWN OF CUSTODIAL/REHABILITATIVE STAFF AT
EACH OF THE MAXIMUM SECURITY PRISONS
FOR ADULT MALES IN NEW YORK STATE

1959

Prison	Total Personnel		Custody		Rehabili-tation		Other	
	#	%	#	%	#	%	#	%
Attica	441	100	344	78	8	2	89	20
Auburn	372	100	294	79	6	1	72	20
Clinton	457	100	364	80	5	1	88	19
Green Haven	430	100	331	77	7	2	94	21
Sing Sing	464	100	358	77	10	2	96	20
Male medium Security Prison Wallkill	188	100	100	53	25	13	73	37
Total	2,362	100	1,791	76	61	2.5	512	22

Custody includes positions of: Correction Lieutenant, Correction Sergeant, Correction Officer, Correction Captain, Assistant Principal Keeper.

Rehabilitation includes positions of: Guidance Supervisor, Guidance Counselor, Institution Education Supervisor, Senior Institution Teacher, Senior Institution Vocational Instructor, Chaplain (Catholic and Protestant, every prison had two chaplains). In addition to the above, Wallkill also had an Assistant Librarian position.

Other includes positions of Administration (Warden, Deputy Warden, Principal Keeper, Head Clerk and other clerical positions), Accounting and Stores (Account Clerks, Steward, Meat Cutter), Hospital Staff (Physician, Dentist, Pharmacist, Nurse, Lab Technician), Food Preparation and Service (Kitchen Keeper, Cook, Baker), Mechanical Engineering (Electrician, Stationary Engineers, Steam Fireman, Plumber, Sewage Plant Operator), Building Maintenance,(Carpenter, Mason, Painter, Roofer and Tinsmith), Clothing Maintenance (Shoe Maker, Laundry Supervisor, Tailor), Motor Equipment and Transportation (Chauffeur, Truck Driver, Foreman), Farms and Grounds, (Farm Manager, Head Farmer, Farmer).

SOURCE: New York State Executive Budget. Department of Correction. State Purposes Budget for 1959-1960, pp. 151-72.

TABLE 2

PROJECTED/ACTUAL INMATE POPULATION, 1959-1972:
PRISONS FOR ADULT MALES

Year	Projected (estimated)	Actual
1959-60	10,445	9,724
1960-61	9,505	9,628
1961-62	9,675	10,042
1962-63	9,750	10,115
1963-64	10,450	10,294
1964-65	10,580	10,351
1965-66	10,660	10,214
1966-67	10,071	9,825
1967-68	10,180	9,044
1968-69	9,625	8,330
1969-70**	8,700	8,775
1970-71**	9,000	8,820
1971-72**	9,500	9,770

**New York State begins to take New York City inmates to relieve overcrowding in NYC institutions. Discussed in Chapter IV.

New York City Inmates in New York State Institutions

```
1969-70 -   413  (actual)
1970-71 - 2,386  (actual)
1971-72 - 3,000  (estimated)
1972-73 - 3,000  (estimated
```

SOURCE: Executive Budget, New York State, Department of Correction. State Purposes Budget for years 1959-1972.

TABLE 3

BREAKDOWN OF PRISON PERSONNEL: CUSTODIAL, REHABILITATIVE AND OTHER 1959-1973

Year	Total Personnel Maximum Male Institutions		Custody		Rehabilitation		Other	
	No.	%	No.	%	No.	%	No.	%
1959-60	2,362	100	1,791	76	61	2.5	512	22
1960-61	2,342	100	1,774	76	61	3	507	22

Change in Budget Format indicates that figures are only available for total institutional personnel--includes reformatories, women's institutions, hospitals for the criminally insane and work camps.

Year	No.	%	No.	%	No.	%	No.	%
1961-62	6,100	100	4,346	71	331	5	1,423	23
1962-63	6,207	100	4,419	71	356	6	1,432	23
1963-64	6,240	100	4,442	71	374	6	1,424	23
1964-65	6,244	100	4,442	71	378	6	1,424	23

Further change in Budget format--lists only new positions and breakdown is only for adult male prisons.

Year	No.	%	No.	%	No.	%	No.	%
1965-66	2,472	100	48 new positions		12 new positions		--	
1966-67	2,507	100	10 "		5 "		--	
1967-68	2,654	100	-- "		14 "		--	
1968-69	2,689	100	5 "		10 "		--	

1969-70 No new custodial nor rehabilitative positions. Department begins to accept NACC patients--so transfer of custodial positions to NACC budget.

Budget format reverts to method used in 1959-1960.

Year	No.	%	No.	%	No.	%	No.	%
1970-71	2,729	100	2,010	74	159	6	560	21
1971-72	2,802	100	2,064	74	166	6	572	20
1972-73	3,012	100	2,209	73	197	6.5	606	20

SOURCE: New York State Executive Budget. Department of Correction. State Purposes Budget, 1959-1972.

BIBLIOGRAPHY

Books

American Friends Service Committee.
Struggle for Justice. New York: Hill and Wang, 1971.

Atkins, Burton and Glick, Henry.
Prisons, Protests and Politics. Englewood Cliffs, N.J.: Prentice Hall, Inc., 1972.

Attica: The Official Report of the New York State
Special Commission on Attica. (The McKay Commission Report). New York: A Bantam Book, 1972.

Banfield, Edward C.
Political Influence. New York: The Free Press, 1961.

_____.
The Unheavenly City Revisited. Boston: Little, Brown and Company, 1974

Barnes, Harry Elmer.
The Story of Punishment. Montclair, N.J.: Patterson Smith, 1972. Second Edition Revised. (originally published in 1930).

Blumberg, Abraham.
Criminal Justice, Second Edition. New York: New Viewpoints, Franklin Watts Inc., 1979.

Challenge of Crime in a Free Society.
A Report by the President's Commission on Law Enforcement and the Administration of Justice. Washington, D.C.: U.S. Government Printing Office, 1967.

Clark, Richard X.
The Brothers of Attica. New York: Links Books, 1973.

Connery, Robert and Benjamin, Gerald (eds.).
Governing New York State: The Rockefeller Years. Proceedings of the Academy of Political Science, May 1974.

_____.
Rockefeller of New York. Ithaca: Cornell University Press, 1979.

Crouch, Ben ed.
  The Keepers. Springfield, Ill.: Charles C. Thomas, 1980.

Cullen, Francis and Gilbert, Karen.
  Reaffirming Rehabilitation. Cincinnati: Anderson Publishing
  Co., 1982

Dahl, Robert.
  Modern Political Analysis, First Edition, Third Edition,
  Englewood Cliffs, N.J.: Prentice Hall, Inc., 1963, 1976.

_____.
  A Preface to Democratic Theory. Chicago: University of
  Chicago Press, 1956.

_____.
  Who Governs? New Haven: Yale University Press, 1961.

_____. and Lindblom, Charles.
  Politics, Economics and Welfare. New York: Harper and
  Row Publishing Co., 1953.

de Beaumont, Gustave and de Toqueville, Alexis.
  On the Penitentiary System in the United States and It's
  Application in France. Carbondale: Southern Illinois Press,
  1964. (originally published in Philadelphia by Carey, Lea
  and Blanchard, 1833).

Dolbeare, Kenneth and Dolbeare, Patricia.
  American Ideologies. Chicago: Markham Publishing Co.,
  1971.

_____. and Edelman, Murray.
  American Politics. Second Edition. Lexington, Mass.:
  D.C. Heath and Company, 1974.

Domhoff, G. William.
  The Higher Circles: The Governing Class in America. New
  York: Random House, 1970.

Edelman, Murray.
  The Symbolic Uses of Politics. Chicago: University of
  Illinois Press, 1967.

_____.
  Politics as Symbolic Action. Chicago: Markham Publishing
  Company, 1971.

Elder, Charles and Cobb, Roger.
   The Political Uses of Symbols. New York: Longman Inc.,
   1983.

Foucault, Michel.
   Discipline and Punish. New York: Vintage Books, Random
   House, Inc., 1979.

_____.
   I, Pierre Riviere. Lincoln: University of Nebraska Press,
   1982, 1975.

Frankel, Marvin.
   Criminal Sentences. New York: Hill and Wang, 1972.

Gaylin, Willard.
   The Killing of Bonnie Garland. New York: Penguin Books,
   1983.

Gerber, Rudolph and McAnany, Patrick (eds.).
   Contemporary Punishment. Notre Dame: Notre Dame
   University Press, 1972.

Gerth, H. H. and Mills, C. Wright.
   From Max Weber: Essays in Sociology. New York: Oxford
   University Press, 1946.

Greenberg, David, (ed.).
   Crime and Capitalism. Palo Alto, Calif.: Mayfield
   Publishing Co., 1981.

Gusfield, Joseph.
   Symbolic Crusade. Chicago: University of Illinois Press,
   1963 (Fourth printing 1976).

Haft, Marilyn and Hermann, Michele.
   Prisoners' Rights. Vols. 1 and 2. New York: Practicing
   Law Institute, 1972.

Halebsky, Sandor.
   Mass Society and Political Conflict. Cambridge: Cambridge
   University Press, 1976.

Hazelrigg, Lawrence, (ed.).
   Prison Within Society. Garden City: Doubleday and Co.,
   Anchor Books, 1968.

Hollingshead, August B., and Redlich, Fredrich C.
   Social Class and Mental Illness. New York: John Wiley and
   Sons, 1958.

Inciardi, James.
    Criminal Justice. New York: Academic Press, 1984.

Jacobs, James B.
    New Perspectives on Prisons and Imprisonment. Ithaca:
    Cornell University Press, 1983.

Killinger, George G. et al. (eds.).
    Penology: The Evolution of Corrections in America. New
    York: West Publishing Co., 1979.

Lewis, W. David.
    From Newgate to Dannemora: The Rise of the Penitentiary
    in New York 1796-1848. Ithaca: Cornell University Press,
    1965.

Lindblom, Charles.
    The Intelligence of Democracy. New York: Macmillan Press,
    1965.

Lipsky, Michael.
    Protest in City Politics. Chicago: Rand McNally and
    Company, 1970.

MacCormick, Austin.
    The Education of Adult Prisoners. New York: National
    Society of Penal Information, 1931.

McConnell, Grant.
    Private Power and American Democracy. New York: Vintage
    Books, 1966.

McGee, Richard A.
    Prisons and Politics. Lexington, Mass.: D.C. Heath and
    Co., 1981.

McKelvey, Blake.
    American Prisons. Montclair, N.J.: Patterson Smith, 1968.

Matthews, Donald R.
    The Social Background of Political Decision Makers. Garden
    City: Doubleday and Co., 1954.

Menninger, Karl.
    The Crime of Punishment. New York: The Viking Press,
    1969.

Mills, C. Wright.
    The Sociological Imagination. New York: Oxford University
    Press, 1959.

Oswald, Russell G.
    Attica, My Story.   Garden City; Doubleday and Co., 1972.

Parenti, Michael.
    Democracy for The Few.   New York: St. Martin's Press,
    1974.

Platt, Anthony.
    The Child Savers.   Chicago: The University of Chicago
    Press, 1969.

_____.
    The Politics of Riot Commissions.   New York: Collier Books,
    1971.

Polsby, Nelson.
    Community Power and Political Theory.   New Haven: Yale
    University Press, 1963.

Quinney, Richard.
    Criminology.   Second Edition.   Boston: Little, Brown and
    Company, 1979.

_____.
    Class, State and Crime.   Second Edition.   New York:
    Longman Inc., 1980.

Radzinowicz, Leon.
    Ideology and Crime.   New York: Columbia Univeristy Press,
    1966.

_____. and Wolfgang, Marvin (eds.).
    Crime and Justice.   vols. 1-3.   Second and Revised
    Edition.   New York: Basic Books, 1977.

Rothman, David J.
    The Discovery of The Asylum.   Boston: Little, Brown and
    Company, 1971.

_____.
    Conscience and Convenience.   Boston: Little, Brown and
    Company, 1980.

Schattschneider, E.E.
    The Semi Sovereign People.   New York: Holt, Rinehart and
    Winston, 1960.

Schwartz, Martin et al. (eds.).
    Corrections: An Issues Approach.   Cincinnati: Anderson
    Publishing Co., 1980.

Stastny, Charles and Tyrnauer, Gabrielle.
  Who Rules the Joint? Lexington: D.C. Heath and Company,
  1982.

Sykes, Gresham.
  The Society of Captives. Princeton: Princeton University
  Press, 1958.

Truman, David.
  The Governmental Process. New York: Knopf Publishing
  Co., 1951.

Wicker, Tom.
  A Time To Die. New York: Quadrangle/The New York
  Times Book Company, 1975.

Wright, Erik Olin.
  The Politics of Punishment. New York: Harper and Row,
  Publishers, 1973.

Articles

Barnett, Richard J.
  "The National Security Managers and the National Interest."
  Politics and Society.1 (February 1971).

Benjamin, Gerald.
  "Patterns in New York State Politics." in Governing New
  York State:The Rockefeller Years, pp. 31-44. Edited by
  Robert Connery and Gerald Benjamin. New York: The
  Academy of Political Science, 1974.

Chartock, Alan.
  "Narcotic Addiction: The Politics of Frustration." in
  Governing New York State: The Rockefeller Years, pp.
  239-49. Edited by Robert Connery and Gerald Benjamin.
  New York: The Academy of Political Science, 1974.

Connery, Robert.
  "Nelson A. Rockefeller as Governor." in Governing New
  York State: The Rockefeller Years, pp. 1-15. Edited by
  Robert Connery and Gerald Benjamin. New York: The
  Academy of Political Science, 1974.

Gans Herbert.
  "The Positive Functions of Poverty." American Journal of
  Sociology, 78:2 (September 1972): pp. 275-89.

Grusky, Oscar.
"Role Conflict in Organization: A Study of Prison Camp
Officials." in Prison Within Society, pp. 455-76. Edited by
Lawrence Hazelrigg. Garden City: Doubleday and
Company, Anchor Books, 1968.

Lipsky, Michael.
"Protest as Political Resource." American Political Science
Review, 62 (December 1968); pp. 1144-58.

Lindquist, Charles.
"Inmate Self Government and Grievance Resolution: Prison
Reform Through Inmate Participation." in Penology: The
Evolution of Corrections in America pp. 215-31. Edited by
George Killinger et al. New York: West Publishing, 1979.

Lowi, Theodore.
"American Business, Public Policy: Case Studies and
Political Theory." World Politics 16:4 (July 1964).
Princeton: Princeton University Press.

MacNamara, Donal.
"The Medical Model in Corrections: Requiescat in Pace." in
Corrections:An Issues Approach pp.176-82. Edited by
Martin Schwartz et al. Cincinnati: Anderson Publishing
Company, 1980.

Milleman, Michael.
"Prison Disciplinary Hearings and Procedural Due Process-
The Requirement of a Full Administrative Hearing." in
Prisoners' Rights, pp. 149-81. Edited by Marilyn Haft and
Michele Hermann. Vol 2. New York: Practicing Law
Institute, 1972.

Mitford, Jessica.
"Kind and Usual Punishment in California." in Prisons,
Protest and Politics. pp. 151-167. Edited by Burton
Atkins and Henry Glick. Englewood Cliffs, N.J.: Prentice
Hall, Inc., 1972.

Petchesky, Rosalind.
"At Hard Labor: Penal Confinement and Production in
Nineteenth Century America." in Crime and Capitalism. pp.
341-57. Edited by David Greenberg. Palo Alto: Mayfield
Publishing Company, 1981.

Puckett, Myron.
"Successful Protest Movements in School Districts." Urban
Education. (April 1976): 31-47.

Stotland, Ezra.
"Self-Esteem and Violence by Guards and State Troopers at Attica." in The Keepers. pp. 291-301. Edited by Ben Crouch. Springfield: Charles C. Thomas, Publisher, 1980.

Turner, William.
"Establishing the Rule of Law in Prisons: A Manual for Prisoners' Rights Litigation." in Prisoners' Rights, pp. 69-114. Edited by Marilyn Haft and Michele Hermann. Vol. 1. New York: Practicing Law Institute, 1972.

Williams, Frank.
"The Demise of the Criminological Imagination: A Critique of Recent Criminology." in Justice Quarterly 1:1 (March 1984) pp.91-106.

Willis, Cecil L.
"Criminal Justice Theory: A Case of Trained Incapacity." in Journal of Criminal Justice 11:5 (1983) pp. 447-458.

Witt, Stuart.
"Modernizing the Legislature." in Governing New York State: The Rockefeller Years, pp.45-57. Edited by Robert Connery and Gerald Benjamin. New York: The Academy of Political Science, 1974.

Zald, Meyer N.
"Power Balance and Staff Conflict in Correctional Institutions." in Prison Within Society. pp. 397-425. Edited by Lawrence Hazelrigg. Garden City: Doubleday and Company, Anchor Books, 1968.

Book Reviews

Bennis, Warren.
Review of Symbolic Uses of Politics, by Murray Edelman, Annals of the American Academy, 361 (September 1965): 142-43.

Davis, James C.
Review of Symbolic Uses of Politics, by Murray Edelman, American Political Science Review, 59:3 (September 1965): 695-96.

Lasswell, Harold.
Review of Symbolic Uses of Politics, by Murray Edelman, American Journal of Sociology, 70:6 (May 1965) :735.

Review of Symbolic Uses of Politics, by Murray Edelman, London
Times Literary Supplement, 22 April 1965, p. 309.

Reports

Annual Report of the New York Department of Efficiency and
Economy. Albany: J.B. Lyon Co., 1915.

Governor Nelson A. Rockefeller's Conference on Crime.
Proceedings, New York City, December 15, 1967, April 21-22,
1966.

Legislative Memoranda. New York Urban Coalition, 1971-73.

Manual for the Use of the Legislature of the State of New York
by John P. Lomenzo, Secretary of the State. New York State
Publication, 1970.

Messages of the Governor Nelson A. Rockefeller to the State of
New York Legislature, 1960-73.

New York State Executive Budgets. Department of Correction.
State Purposes and Capital Construction Budgets, 1959-60 through
1984-85. New York State Publications.

New York State Legislative Annual, 1960-73.

New York State Legislative Program for 1973. Publication by the
Committee on Public Affairs, Community Service Society. New
York, January 1973.

Office of Legislative Research Fact Sheets, Crime, Corrections
and Criminal Justice, 1966-73. Office of Legislative Research.
Albany, New York.

Preliminary Report of the Governor's Special Committee on
Criminal Offenders. New York State Publication, June 1968.

Public Hearings of the New York State Special Commission on
Attica, WNET Broadcast (channel 13), April 1972. (Personal tape
recording)

Report of the Commission to Investigate Prison Administration and
Construction. New York State Publication. Albany, New York,
February 15, 1931.

Report of the Commission to Investigate Prison Administration and
Construction. Educational Program Report. New York State

163

Publication. Albany, New York. January 1932.

Seventh Interim Report of the State of New York Temporary Commission on Revision of the Penal Law and Criminal Code, April 1, 1968 Legislative Document (1968) Number 29.

1967 Youth and Correction Legislation in New York State. Report of the Committee on Youth and Correction of the Community Service Society, September 1967.

Attica 1982 An Analysis of the Current Conditions in New York State Prisons. A Report of the Correctional Association of New York. September 1982.

Crime and Punishment in New York. An Inquiry into Sentencing and the Criminal Justice System. Report to Governor Hugh L. Carey by the Executive Advisory Committee on Sentencing. March 1979.

The Rehabilitation of Criminal Offenders: Problems and Prospects. Edited by Lee Sechrest et al. Panel on Research on Rehabilitative Techniques. Washington, D.C.: National Academy of Sciences Publications. 1979.

1980-1985 New York State Department of Correctional Services Master Plan. New York State Publication. January 1981.

Unpublished Materials

Alliance for a Safer New York. Legislative Memoranda, 1972-73. (Mimeograph).

A Review of Various Aspects of the New York State Correctional Program. A Report to the New York Legislature by the Senate Finance Minority. Samuel Greenberg, Chairman. (Greenberg Report) August 29, 1971. (Mimeograph).

Governor's Crime Control Program. Report of the Office of Legislative Research, April 9, 1968. (Mimeograph).

Minutes of the Proceedings of Budget Hearings on the Department of Correction held by the Senate Committee on Finance and the Assembly Ways and Means Committee in the Assembly Parlor, Capitol Building, Albany, New York. February 29, 1968; February 16, 1970; February 10, 1971; February 29, 1972. (Mimeograph).

Public Hearing in New York City by the Governor's Special Committee on Criminal Offenders. Hearing Report - Untitled and with no date. (Mimeograph).

Report of the Senate Committee on Penal Institutions for the 1967 Legislative Session, March 30, 1967. (Mimeograph).

Transcript of the Hearing of the New York State Senate Committee on Penal Institutions on Work Release Legislation, March 28, 1968, Albany New York. (Mimeograph).

WCBS Television Broadcast, August 31, 1969 at 11:30 A.M. Interview with George McGrath, New York City Commissioner of Correction and John R. Dunne, New York State Senator. "New York City's Overcrowded Jails." (Transcript).

Interviews

Burleigh, Gladys.
  Staff Associate, National Conference of Christians and Jews, New York City, March 1975.

Clifford, Donald.
  Staff Associate and author of the Greenberg Report, Senate Minority Finance Committee, in Albany, New York, February 28, 1975.

Corrigan, John.
  Staff Associate, Division of the Budget. Albany, New York, March 21, 1975.

Coughlin, Thomas.
  Commissioner of the Department of Correctional Services in New York State. Albany, New York. June 27, 1984.

Delaney, John.
  Former Assistant Director of the Governor's Special Committee on Criminal Offenders, in New York City, December 1, 1974.

Dunbar, Walter.
  Former Deputy Commissioner of the New York State Department of Correctional Services, Albany, New York, May 29, 1974.

Dunne, John R.
  New York State Senator, former Chairman of the New York

165

State Senate Standing Committee on Penal Institutions, March 17, 1975, Albany, New York.

Feingold, Polly.
Former Legislative Representative, New York Urban Coalition, New York, May 1974.

Fitzgerald, Matthew.
Former New York State Director of the National Council on Crime and Delinquency, Albany, New York, March 20, 1975.

Goff, Donald.
Former General Secretary of the Correctional Association of New York, October 1972-April 1973.

Kernohan, Frances.
Staff Associate, Community Service Society in New York City, March 3, 1975.

MacCormick, Austin.
President of the Osborne Association, in New York City, May 2, 1974.

McEvoy, Don.
National Conference of Christians and Jews, Staff Associate, New York City, March 1975.

McKendrick, Charles.
Former Warden, Wallkill Prison, in Wallkill, New York, December 17-18, 1968.

Oswald, Russell G.
Former Commissioner of the Department of Correctional Services, Albany, New York, March 19, 1975.

Roos, David.
Staff Associate Minority Finance Committee in the New York State Senate, Albany, New York, October 1974.

Rosado, Henry.
Correction Officer, Downstate Correctional Facility, New York State, in Poughkeepsie, New York. April 1984.

Ternullo, Vito.
Former Director of the Division of Education in the New York State Department of Correction, in Elmira, New York, May 9-10, 1974.

Newspapers

A general survey of the following newspapers from October 1968-1973.

Buffalo Evening News
Christian Science Monitor
Citizen Advertiser (Auburn, New York)
Daily News (New York City)
Long Island Press
New York Post
The New York Times
Newsday (Long Island)
Rochester Democrat
The Schenectady Gazette
Sunday News (New York City)
Syracuse Post Standard

Participant Observation

Research Assistant to Senator John R. Dunne   1968-1970

Special Assistant to the Director of the Women's Unit, Governor's Office, New York and Albany, 1970-1972.

Assistant Director, Alliance for a Safer New York, 1972-1973.

Board Member, Women's Prison Association, 1970-1974.

About the Author

The author was born in New York City and received her Doctor of Philosophy degree in Political Science from Fordham University in 1978. Her previous degrees were also earned at Fordham University.

Subsequent employment included positions with the office of State Senator John R. Dunne, (Research Assistant); the Women's Unit, Office of the Governor, (Special Assistant); and the Alliance for a Safer New York, (Assistant Director).

She is currently tenured Associate Professor of Criminal Justice/Political Science at Marist College in Poughkeepsie, New York. She resides with her husband, Dr. James C. Mc Eleney, in New York City.